Germanic Legal Codes

Table of Contents

Aldii 1
Code of Euric 1
Code of Leovigild 1
Compurgation 2
Danish Code 2
Early Germanic law 4
Edictum Rothari 9
Law of Hlothhere and Eadric 10
Law of Wihtred 11
Law of Æthelberht 12
Lex Alamannorum 13
Lex Baiuvariorum 14
Lex Burgundionum 14
Lex Frisionum 16
Lex Ripuaria 17
Lex Saxonum 17
Norwegian Code 18
Raffelstetten Customs Regulations ... 18
Sachsenspiegel 19
Salic law 20
Schwabenspiegel 23
Visigothic Code 24

Preface

Each chapter in this book ends with a URL to a hyperlinked online version. Use the online version to access related pages, websites, footnotes, tables, color photos, updates, or to see the chapter's contributors. Click the edit link to suggest changes. Please type the URL exactly as it appears. If you change the URL's capitalization, for example, it may not work.

Purchase of this book entitles you to a free trial membership in the publisher's book club at www.booksllc.net. (Time limited offer.) Simply enter the barcode number from the back cover onto the membership form on our home page. The book club entitles you to select from millions of books at no additional charge, including a PDF copy of this and related books to read on the go. Simply enter the title or subject onto the search form to find them.

If you have any questions, could you please be so kind as to consult our Frequently Asked Questions page at www.booksllc.net/faqs.cfm? You are also welcome to contact us there.

Publisher: Books LLC, Wiki Series, Memphis, TN, USA, 2013.

Aldii

Aldii - the semi-free in Germanic law. Employees of a patron, their position was intermediate between freedom and slavery, but ended up sometimes confused with the serfs. Deprived of political and military rights and related to the land they cultivated, could marry and be defended in court, were entitled to wergild (the amount is less than that of the free) and, within limits, to the property.

Source http://en.wikipedia.org/wiki/Aldii

Code of Euric

The **Codex Euricianus** or **Code of Euric** was a collection of laws governing the Visigoths compiled at the order of Euric, King of Spain, sometime before 480, probably at Toulouse (possible at Arles); it is one of the earliest examples of early Germanic law. The compilation itself was the work of Leo, a Roman lawyer and principal counsellor of the king. The customs of the Visigothic nation were recognised and affirmed. The Code is largely confused and it appears that it was merely a recollection of Gothic custom altered by Roman law.

The code entrenches a clear stratification of Gothic and Gallo-Roman society. There is the class of lords, who are called either *domini* or *patroni* depending on whether they were lords of slaves or freemen. And there are two classes of freemen who have lords above them: the *buccellarii* and the *saiones*. The Code was in fact the first legal recognition of the *buccellariatus*, an office which the Roman Emperors were trying to ban. The *buccellarii* were a knightly class, they could change lords, but they had to return all the landed benefices they had received from their former lord.

Source http://en.wikipedia.org/wiki/Code_of_Euric

Code of Leovigild

The **Code of Leovigild** or **Codex Revisus** was a Visigothic legal code, a revision of the Codex Euricianus made in the late sixth century under Leovigild (568–586). The code does not survive and all we know of it is derived from the writings of Isidore of Seville, a near contemporary ecclesiastic and encyclopaedist. Nevertheless, it was the Gothic basis of the later Liber Iudiciorum, an Iberian law code which united it with the law code of the Hispano-Roman population, the Breviary of Alaric.

In 1974, García Gallo made a critical examination of the evidence for the code and came to reject the claim of Isidore that Leovigild had formulated a new code, since the laws of Chindasuinth dictated modifications to laws more ancient the reign of Leovigild.

Navigation menu

Personal tools

Create account
Log in

Namespaces

Article
Talk

Variants

Actions

Search

Navigation

Main page
Contents
Featured content
Current events
Random article
Donate to Wikipedia

Interaction

Help
About Wikipedia
Community portal
Recent changes
Contact Wikipedia

Toolbox

What links here
Related changes

Upload file
Special pages
Permanent link
Page information
Cite this page

Print/export

Create a book
Download as PDF
Printable version

Languages

Català
Español
Italiano
Edit links
Source   http://en.wikipedia.org/wiki/Code_of_Leovigild

Compurgation

Compurgation, also called wager of law, is a defence used primarily in medieval law. A defendant could establish his innocence or nonliability by taking an oath and by getting a required number of persons, typically twelve, to swear they believed the defendant's oath. From Latin, *com* = with, *purgare* = make clean, cleanse, excuse L. *com* is also an intensifier and turns a word into the superlative form, so compurgation, by etymology, means 'to thoroughly clean or excuse'.

Compurgation was found in early Germanic law, in Welsh law, and in the English ecclesiastical courts until the 17th century. In common law it was substantially abolished as a defence in felonies by the Constitutions of Clarendon in 1164. The defence was still permitted in civil actions for debt and vestiges of it survived until statutory repeal at various times in common law countries, e.g. in England in 1833, and Queensland, Australia at some point before the Queensland Common Practice Act of 1867.

Wager of law (compurgation) survived to recent centuries, and, in many jurisdictions has been repealed by statute. An example of this is the Queensland Common Law Practice Act 1867, s 3., which makes direct reference to the abolition of wager of law.

"Wager of Law, obsolete for centuries" ... was "a living fossil ... a dead letter statute" and was repealed in England in 1833.

Source   http://en.wikipedia.org/wiki/Compurgation

Danish Code

Danske Lov (*English*: **Danish Code**) is the title of a Danish statute book from 1683, that previously formed the basis for the Danish legislation. Even though it is mainly a compilation of older, regional laws, it took 7 different commissions several decades under two different monarchs to put the Code together. In 1687, Norway received its Norwegian Code, which in form and content is about identical with Danish Code. Danish Code has been translated into English, Latin, German and Russian.

The statute needs to be viewed in connection with the European traditions of justice, which since the 12th century has moved towards an assembly of different practices. This tradition was encouraged by the Catholic church. The majority of the statute has now been superseded by newer laws. However, parts of the Code still apply, e.g. 3-19-2, which states that an employer is responsible for compensation for damages that an employee might incur during his employment.

Background

The historical book Gesta Danorum by Saxo Grammaticus, which is dated to the 13th century, describes the Danish kings' attempts at legislation. One of the first examples of Danish legislation was 'Vederloven' from the 1180s, that regulated the personal army of the king, also known as the Housecarls. This was superseded by a series of regional laws, first Scanian Law, later Jyske Lov and Sjællandske Lov. Generally, the regional laws are based on Casuistry. This means that they are based on concrete cases of breaches of the law, and describe how the conflict is to be solved. However, the rules of procedure are broad.

History

The two first Law Committees and Peder Lassen

Christian V of Denmark

Immediately after gaining absolute power King Frederick III appointed a commission to scrutinize the laws of the kingdom, to identify laws that were in conflict with the absolute power of the king and to work out a new procedure for the administration of justice. Danish Code is seen as being born of necessity, as justice was at the time administered on the basis of a large number of somewhat contradictory laws.

Additionally, the division of Denmark into two judiciary areas, based on Jutland and Zealand respectively was seen as bothersome and anachronistic. On January 12, 1661, the State College (Danish: 'Statskollegiet'), a governing body overseeing the workings of the government, published a report suggesting to work out a comprehensive Danish Code. King Frederick III then established The First Law Committee consisting of 3 jurists (including Supreme Court Assessor Peder Lassen), 8 noblemen and 10 civilians. Work in the first Committee broke down, one of the causes being that the noblemen were unhappy with the suggested diminishing of their privileges.

On November 16, 1662, the King replaced the first Committee with the Second Law Committee consisting of the former Committee's four foremost legal experts, Peder Lassen, Heinrich Ernst, Otte Krag and Niels Trolle. The Committee drafted several completely new statutes, and especially Peder Lassens suggestions regarding inheritance were ahead of their time in Denmark. The Committee's suggestions regarding laws of legal procedure were handed to the State College, which replied positively in July, 1664. To revise the suggestions, the Second Law Committee was expanded with four jurists from the State College, after which the work began to decline once again.

The third Law Committee and Rasmus Vinding

A third Committee was established on February 23, 1666, consisting of Peder Lassen, Vice Treasurer Holger Vind, State College Assessor Kristoffer Parsberg and Supreme Court judge Rasmus Vinding. The new Committee reflected the influence of statesman Peder Schumacher (Count Griffenfeld after his ennoblement), as both Parsberg and Vinding were his close friends. The third Committee started off a lengthy conflict between Lassen and Vinding regarding the Code, as Lassen was the professional jurist, while Vinding lacked legal training. A professor of history and geography, Vinding had a good reputation as a gifted judge, but lacked in-depth knowledge of the Danish laws.

Work in the Third Committee did not get under way, so on March 8, 1666, the King ordered each of the Committee's four members to compile and revise their own set of laws, removing outdated statutes from the Danish system of legal writs. In practice, all earlier work was abandoned, which was a defeat for Lassen who had been the driving force so far, and perhaps a tactical move by the King to have him superseded by Vinding. Of the four submitted drafts, Vinding's so-called *Codex Fredericus* gained the best reception, after which legislative work dwindled down again. Meanwhile Lassen kept his rejected draft at hand should Vinding's draft be turned down.

By the late 1660s, Vinding's friend Peder Schumacher was appointed as Assessor both to the State College and the Supreme Court. He used his influence with the King to get Vinding's draft approved, so Vinding by a secret order on March 11, 1669 was given the task of drafting the new body of laws, *Corpus juris Danici*. By the end of 1669, Vinding put forth his suggestions, which was an updated version of his earlier *Codex Fredericus*, but with a more systematic setup and fewer outdated or contradictory sections. The content of the text was mainly old laws coupled with new laws based on earlier verdicts (i.e. Common Law).

Revisions under Christian V

After the death of King Frederick III in 1670, legislative work slowed down again. Peder Schumacher's (now Count Griffenfeld) interest in the project also died down.

First Committee: After a long break, on September 24, 1672 a three-person Revision Committee was established to revise Rasmus Vindings draft. The three members were Peder Lassen, Attorney General Peder Lauridsen Scavenius and chancellor Peder Reedtz, who headed the committee. Bishop Hans Vandal was also connected to the work, revising the sections dealing with the clergy. Lassen criticized Vinding's division of the Code into five parts, suggesting only three parts instead. However, his criticism was not as vehement as previously, perhaps because he tired out – Lassen had been connected with the project since its beginning 11 years earlier. Lassen's revisions to the draft are mostly corrections of misunderstandings, with very few highly negative comments. Thus, Vinding and Griffenfeld (previously Schumacher) had won the battle over the layout of the text.

Second Committee: With the death of committee leader Reedz on July 10, 1674, Griffenfeld took over. He created the Second Revision Committee by including his brother-in-law, mayor of Copenhagen Jørgen Fogh and his friend Vinding in the committee. When Griffenfeld fell from power on March 11, 1676, work on the Danish Code stopped completely for four years.

Third Committee: On February 28, 1680, a royal missive was published establishing the Third Revision Committee. It consisted of 13 members, among these the three clergymen bishop Hans Bagger, Royal Confessor Hans Leth and professor in theology Kristian Nold. Work in the committee broke down, mainly because of the clergymen who unsuccessfully tried to demolish the committee. The sticking point was the rights of confession of foreigners living in Denmark, especially the exiled French Huguenots.

Fourth Committee: The drawn out arguments caused the King to appoint a Fourth Revision Committee on April 16, 1681, consisting of four people, among these Rasmus Vinding. They were selected to complete a final revision of the Code, and they made many minor changes and additions to the previous draft. The committee completed its work by the end of 1681, and the King approved the Danish Code on January 3, 1682. Small corrections continued to be made until June 23, where the Law was printed, even though it was officially completed on April 15, the King's birthday.

Contents

In addition to the oaths sworn by judges and witnesses, Danish code contains six books:
1: Om Retten og Rettens Personer (The court and people at the court)
2: Om Religion og Geistligheden (Religion and the clergy)
3: Om Verdslig- og Huus-Stand (Temporal positions)
4: Om Søretten (The Maritime Court)
5: Om Adkomst, Gods og Gield (Inheritance, estate and debt)
6: Om Misgierninger (Misdeeds)

Implication and importance of the Code

The final Danish Code is first and foremost based on earlier Danish legislative work. Roman law, which held great influence in Europe at the time, can only be traced in a few places. This fits well with the main purpose, which since the Third Law Committee was to compile already existing laws into a more useful format. Thus, Danish Code only treated new areas to a limited extent.

Later professors of law and history, notably Anders Sandøe Ørsted and Edvard Holm, have commented that the Danish Code was one particularly positive aspect of the absolute monarchy, although Stig Iuul holds that earlier legislation deserves the credit because Danish Code is mostly a compilation.

The English envoy to Denmark at the time, Robert Molesworth, praises the Danish Code in his otherwise highly negative text, *An account of Denmark as it was in the year 1692*. He states that in justice, brevity and clarity, the Code surpasses all other legal texts he knows of. It is so clear and simple to understand, that any literate person can understand his case and is able to represent himself in Court if he so wishes.

Source http://en.wikipedia.org/wiki/Danish_Code

Early Germanic law

Several Latin **law codes** of the **Germanic peoples** written in the **Early Middle Ages** (also known as *leges barbarorum* "laws of the barbarians") survive, dating to between the 5th and 9th centuries. They are influenced by Roman law, ecclesiastical law, and earlier tribal customs.

Germanic law was codified in writing under the influence of Roman law; previously it was held in the memory of designated individuals who acted as judges in confrontations and meted out justice according to customary rote, based on careful memorization of precedent. Among the Franks they were called *rachimburgs*. "Living libraries, they were law incarnate, unpredictable and terrifying." When justice is oral, the judicial act is personal and subjective. Power, whose origins were at once magical, divine and military, as Michel Rouche has pointed out, was exercised jointly by the "throne-worthy" elected king and his free warrior companions. Oral law sufficed as long as the warband was not settled in one place. Germanic law made no provisions for the public welfare, the *res publica* of Romans

The principal examples are:
Code of Euric, (Visigoths) - c. 480
Lex Burgundionum, (Burgundians, Gundobad) - c. 500
Lex Salica (Salian Franks, Clovis I) - c. 500
Pactus Alamannorum (Alamanni) - c. 620
Lex Ripuaria (Ripuarian Franks) - 630s
Edictum Rothari (Lombards, Rothari) - 643
Lex Visigothorum (Visigoths, Recceswinth) - 654
Lex Alamannorum (Alamanni) - 730
Lex Bajuvariorum (Bavarians) - c. 745
Lex Frisionum (Frisians) - c. 785
Lex Saxonum (Saxons) - 803
Lex Angliorum et Werinorum, hoc est, Thuringorum - 9th century
The language of all these continental codes was Latin; the only known codes drawn up in any Germanic language were the Anglo-Saxon laws, beginning with the Laws of Æthelberht (7th century). In the 13th century customary Saxon law was codified in the vernacular as the *Sachsenspiegel*.

All these laws may be described in general as codes of governmental procedure and tariffs of compositions. They all present somewhat similar features with Salic law, the best-known example, but often differ from it in the date of compilation, the amounts of fines, the number and nature of the crimes, the number, rank, duties and titles of the officers, etc.

In Germanic Europe in the Early Middle Ages, every man was tried according to the laws of his own race, whether Roman, Salian or Ripuarian Frank, Burgundian, Visigoth, Bavarian etc.

A number of separate codes were drawn up specifically to deal with cases between ethnic Romans. These codes differed from the normal ones that covered cases between Germanic peoples, or between Germanic people and Romans. The most notable of these are the *Lex Romana Visigothorum* or *Breviary of Alaric* (506), the *Lex Romana Curiensis* and the *Lex Romana Burgundionum*.

Tacitus

Tacitus in his *Germania* gives an account of the legal practice of the Germanic peoples of the 1st century. Tacitus reports that criminal cases were put before the thing (tribal assembly). Lighter offenses were regulated with damages (paid in livestock), paid in part to the victim (or their family) and in part to the king. The death penalty is reserved for two kinds of capital offenses: military treason or desertion was punished by hanging, and moral infamy (cowardice and homosexuality) was punished by throwing the condemned into a bog. The difference in punishment is explained by the idea that "glaring iniquities" must be exposed in plain sight, while "effeminacy and pollution" should best be buried and concealed. Minor legal disputes were settled on a day-to-day basis by elected chiefs assisted by elected officials.

Principles

The Germanic law codes are designed for a clearly stratified society fixated on kinship. Legal status, and therefore freedom, was based on a person's kinship, separating those who have a kindred, or freemen (OE *freo man*, OHG *frīhals*), and those who are kinless, or bondmen (ON *þræll*). Kinship was the basis for e.g. conveying and inheriting property, regulation of feuds, and weregeld, and so bondmen were *ipso facto* excluded from these things. At the head of the freemen was the king with the most rights and privileges. Under the king came the highborn nobility (OE *æþelu*, OS *aðali*, Germ *Adel*) and the warrior class (OE *eorl*, OS/OHG *erl*, ON *jarl*), below the nobility the ordinary freemen (OE *ċeorl*, Frankish *baro*, Burgundian *leudis*), and under the freemen the servant class: freedmen (OE *læt*, *freolæta*, MDu *laet*, *vrilaet*, ON *leysingr*) and slaves (OE *þēow*, OHG *dio*, ON *þýr*, Goth *þius*). This system was augmented by incorporating a separate class of clergy, among whom the bishops were as a rule considered of equal status as a nobleman.

The Germanic law system is in principle based on compensation rather than revenge. Any injury must be compensated according to the damage done, regardless of motive or intent. Even for capital crimes like murder, the compensation is a weregeld, a fixed amount depending on the sex and social status of the victim. The practice of paying part of the damages to the king survives in the earliest Anglo-Saxon law code (Laws of Æthelberht of Kent), under the term *drihtinbeah*, but seems to have been discontinued after Christianisation. As thralls are considered the property of their lord, crimes committed by thralls must be compensated by their owner just like damage caused by animals.

The most extreme punishment for crimes considered irredeemable seems to be outlawry, i.e. the declaration of the guilty party as beyond the protection of the law.

In most instances this may have been equivalent to a death sentence in practice, but the actual death penalty seems to have been foreseen only for very rare cases, such as sexual crimes (incest or homosexuality), religious crimes or crimes against the king, and not necessarily even in such cases. Alamannic law also foresees the death penalty for plotting to assassinate the duke, and for military treason (assisting enemies or causing rebellion in the army), but in these cases the penalty may also be outlawry or a fine, depending on the judgement of the duke or the chieftains.

The weregeld was set at a basic amount of 200 shillings, which could be multiplied depending on the status of the victim. In Anglo-Saxon law, the regular freeman is known as a *two-hynde man* ("a man worth 200"), and noblemen are either *six-hynde man* (threefold weregeld) or *twelve-hynde man* (sixfold weregeld). In Alamannic law, the basic weregeld for a freeman is likewise 200 shillings. Alamannic tradition is particular in doubling the fee if the victim was a woman, so that the weregeld for a free woman is 400 shillings. The weregeld for a priest is threefold, i.e. 600 shillings. Alamannic law further introduces the concept of premeditated murder (as opposed to deaths by accident or in combat), which is fined by ninefold weregeld. The Anglo-Saxon *Norðleoda laga* ("North-people's law") is unique in setting an explicit amount for a king's weregeld, at 30,000 tremisses, explaining that 15,000 tremises is for the man (the same amount as for an atheling or an archbishop) and another 15,000 for the damage to the kingdom.

Unlike Roman law, Germanic law mentions cruentation as a means to prove guilt or innocence.

Individual law codes

Visigothic law codes

Compared with other barbarian tribes, the Goths had the longest time of contact with Roman civilization, from migration in 376 to trade interactions years beforehand. The Visigothic legal attitude held that laws were created as new offenses of justice arose, and that the king's laws originated from God and His justice-scriptural basis. Mercifulness (*clementia*) and a paternal feeling (*pietas*) were qualities of the king exhibited through the laws. The level of severity of the law was "tempered" by this mercy, specifically for the poor; it was thought that by showing paternal love in formation of law, the legislator gained the love of citizen. While the monarch position was implicitly supreme and protected by laws, even kings were subject to royal law, for royal law was thought of as God's law. In theory, enforcement of the law was the duty of the king, and as the sovereign power he could ignore previous laws if he desired, which often led to complications. To regulate the king's power, all future kings took an oath to uphold the law. While the Visigoths' law code reflected many aspects of Roman law, over time it grew to define a new society's requirements and opinions of law's significance to a particular people.

It is certain that the earliest written code of the Visigoths dates to Euric (471). Code of Euric (*Codex Euricianus*), issued between 471 and 476, has been described as "the best legislative work of the fifth century". It was created to regulate the Romans and Goths living in Euric's kingdom, where Romans greatly outnumbered Goths. The code borrowed heavily from the Roman Theodosian Code (*Codex Theodosianus*) from the early 5th century, and its main subjects were Visigoths living in Southern France. It contained about 350 clauses, organized by chapter headings; about 276 to 336 of these clauses remain today. Besides his own constitutions, Euric included in this collection the unwritten constitutions of his predecessors Theodoric I (419-451), Thorismund (451-453), and Theodoric II (453-466), and he arranged the whole in a logical order. Of the Code of Euric, fragments of chapters 276 to 337 have been discovered in a palimpsest manuscript in the Bibliothèque Nationale at Paris (Latin coll, No. 12161), proving that the code ran over a large area. Euric's code was used for all cases between Goths, and between them and Romans; in cases between Romans, Roman law was used.

At the insistence of Euric's son, Alaric II, an examination was made of the Roman laws in use among Romans in his dominions, and the resulting compilation was approved in 506 at an assembly at Aire, in Gascony, and is known as the Breviary of Alaric, and sometimes as the *Liber Aniani*, from the fact that the authentic copies bear the signature of the *referendarius* Anian. organized by chapter headings; about 276 to 336 of these clauses remain today. In 506 CE, Alaric II, son of Euric, assembled the council of Agde to issue the Breviary of Alaric (*Lex Romana Visigothorum*), applying specifically to Hispano-Roman residents of the Iberian Peninsula, where Alaric had migrated the Visigoth population. Both the Code of Euric and Breviary of Alaric borrowed heavily from the Theodosian Code. Euric, for instance, forbad intermarriage between Goths and Romans, which was already expressed in the *Codex Theodosianus*.

Euric's code remained in force among the Visigothic Kingdom of Hispania (the Iberian Peninsula) until the reign of Liuvigild (568-586), who made a new one, the Codex Revisus, improving upon that of his predecessor. This work is lost, and we have no direct knowledge of any fragment of it. In the 3rd codification, however, many provisions have been taken from the 2nd, and these are designated by the word *antiqua*; by means of these *antiqua* we are enabled in a certain measure to reconstruct the work of Leovigild.

After the reign of Leovigild, the legislation of the Visigoths underwent a transformation. New laws made by the kings were declared to be applicable to all subjects in the kingdom, of whatever race; in other words, they became territorial; and this principle of territoriality was gradually extended to the ancient code. Moreover, the conversion of Reccared (586-601) from Arianism to orthodox Christianity effaced the religious differences among his subjects, and all subjects, being Christians, had to submit to the canons of the councils, made obligatory by the kings.

In 643, Visigoth king Chindasuinth (642-653) proposed a new Visigothic Code, the *Lex Visigothorum* (also called the *Liber Iudiciorum* or *Forum Iudicium*), which replaced both the Code of Euric and the Breviary of Alaric. His son, Reccesswinth (649-672), refined this code in its rough form and issued it officially in 654. This code applied equally to both Goths and Romans, presenting "a sign of a new society of Hispania developing in the seventh century, distinctly different from Gothic or Roman". The *Liber Iudiciorum* also marked a shift in the view of the power of law in reference to the king. It stressed that the *Liber Iudiciorum* alone is law, absent of any relation to any kingly authority, instead of the king being the law and the law merely an expression of his decisions. The lacunae in these fragments have been filled by the aid of the law of the Bavarians, where the chief Divisions are reintroduced, divided into 12 books, and subdivided into *tituli* and chapters (*aerae*). It comprises 324 constitutions taken from Leovigild's collection, a few of the laws of Reccared and Sisebur, 99 laws of Chindasuinth, and 87 of Reccasuinth. A recension of this code of Reccasuinth was made in 681 by King Erwig (680-687), and is known as the *Lex Wisigothorum renovate*; and, finally, some *additamenta* were made by Ergica (687-702).

The *Liber Iudiciorum* makes several striking differences from Roman law, especially concerning the issue of inheritance. According to the *Liber Iudiciorum*, if incest is committed, the children can still inherit, whereas in Roman law the children were disinherited and could not succeed. Title II of Book IV outlines the issue of inheritance under the newly united Visigothic Code: section 1, for instance, states that sons and daughters inherit equally if their parents die instate, section 4 says that all family members should inherit if no will exists to express the intentions of the deceased, and the final section expresses a global law of Recceswinth, stating that anyone left without heirs has the power to do what they want with their possessions. This statement recalls the Roman right for a person to leave his possessions to anyone in his will, except this Visigothic law emphasizes males and females equally, whereas, in Roman law, only males (particularly the *pater familias*) are allowed to make a will.

Lex Burgundionum

This is the law code of the Burgundians, probably issued by king Gundobad. It is influenced by Roman law and deals with domestic laws concerning marriage and inheritance as well as regulating weregild and other penalties. Interaction between Burgundians is treated separately from interaction between Burgundians and Gallo-Romans. The oldest of the 14 surviving manuscripts of the text dates to the 9th century, but the code's institution is ascribed to king Gundobad (died 516), with a possible revision by his successor Sigismund (died 523). The *Lex Romana Burgundionum* is a separate code, containing various laws taken from Roman sources, probably intended to apply to the Burgundians' Gallo-Roman subjects. The oldest copy of this text dates to the 7th century.

Lex Salica

The exact origins of the Franks are uncertain: they were a group of Germanic peoples that settled in the lower regions of the Rhine river. They were not a unified people at the start of the 3rd century but consisted of many tribes which were loosely connected with one another. Although they were intertwined with the Roman Empire the Franks were not a part of it. "No large body of Franks was admitted into the Empire, but individuals and small groups did cross." The Romans were seen as a lower rank in Frankish society. With larger numbers the Franks over took the region of the Rhine. Latin became the secondary language to the Germanic one of the Franks and Frankish law took precedence among the people. The Romans even embraced the "Barbarians" to the north at times, making them allies to fight off the Huns.

The Franks were broken down into east and west regions. The Eastern Franks were known as the Ripuarians and those west of the Rhine were known as the Salian Franks. It was King Clovis who united the Franks under one law after defeating his rivals in 509 CE. It is during this time of unification that King Clovis developed the Salic Law.

The Lex Salica was a similar body of law to the Lex Burgundionum. It was compiled between 507 and 511 CE. The body of law deals with many different aspects of Frank society, and through these document historians can discover much about the day to day lives of the Franks. The charges range from inheritance to murder and theft. The Salic law was used to bring order to Frank society, the main punishment for crimes being a fine with a worth designated to the type of crime. The law uses capital punishment only in cases of witchcraft and poisoning. This absence of violence is a unique feature of the Salic Law.

The code was originally brought about by the Frankish King Clovis. The code itself is a blue print for Frankish society and how the social demographics were assembled. One of the main purposes of the Salic Law is to protect a family's inheritance in the agnatic succession. This emphasis on inheritance made the Salic Law a synonym for agnatic succession, and in particular for the "fundamental law" that no woman could be king of France.

The use of fines as the main reparation made it so that those with the money to pay the fine had the ability to get away with the most heinous of crimes. "Those who commit rape shall be compelled to pay 2500 denars, which makes 63 shillings." Rape was not the only detailed violent crime. The murder of children is broken down by age and gender, and so is the murder of women.

Paying fines broke the society into economic and social demographics in that the wealthy were free to do as much as they could afford, whereas the fines themselves placed different values on the gender and racial demographics. This social capital is evident in the differences in the Salic Law's punishment for murder based on a woman's ability to bear children. Women who could bear children were protected by a 600 shilling fine while the fine for murdering a woman who could no longer bear children was only 200 shillings. It is also interesting that all crimes committed against Romans had lesser fines than other social classes. In the case of inheritance, it is made very clear that all property belongs to the males in the family. This also means that all debt also belongs to the males of the family.

The Salic Law outlines a unique way of securing the payment of money owed. It is called the *Chrenecruda* (or *crenecruda, chren ceude, crinnecruda*). In cases where the debtor could not pay back a loan in full they were forced to clear out everything from their home. If the debt still could not be paid off the owner could collect dust from all four corners of the house and cross the threshold. The debtor then turned and face the house with their next of kin gathered behind them. The debtor threw the dust over their shoulder. The person (or persons) that the dust fell upon was then responsible for the payment of the debt. The process continued through the family until the debt was paid. *Chrenecruda* helped secure loans within the Frankish society. It intertwined the loosely gathered tribes and helped to establish government authority. The process made a single person part of a whole group.

The Salic Law helps to show the non-violent side of the *Barbarians*. The Salic Law gave a unique identity and pride to the Franks. Under the Salic law the Franks were able to keep their identity and respect as a society as much of Europe fell under the guidelines of the Burgundian Code.

The Salic Law exists in two forms: the *Pactus Legis Salicae*, which is near to the original form approved by Clovis, and the *Lex Salica*, which is the edited form approved by Charlemagne. Both are published in the Monumenta Germaniae Historica's *Leges* series.

Pactus Alamannorum and Lex Alamannorum

Of the laws of the Alamanni, who dwelt between the Rhine and the Lech, and spread over Alsace and what is now Switzerland to the south of Lake Constance, we possess two different texts.

The earlier text, of which five short fragments have come down to us, is known as the *Pactus Alamannorum*, and judging from the persistent recurrence of the expression *et sic convenit*, was most probably drawn up by an official commission. The reference to *aifranchisement in ecciesia* shows that it was composed after the conversion of the Alamanni to Christianity. There is no doubt that the text dates back at least to the reign of the Frankish king Dagobert I, i.e. to the first half of the 7th century.

The later text, known as the *Lex Alamannorum*, dates from a period when Alamannia was independent under national dukes, but recognized the theoretical suzerainty of the Frankish kings. There seems no reason to doubt the St. Gall manuscript, which states that the law had its origin in an agreement between the great Alamannic lords and Duke Lantfrid, who ruled the duchy from 709 to 730.

Leges Langobardorum

We possess a fair amount of information on the origin of the code of laws of the Lombards. The first part, consisting of 388 chapters, also known as the *Edictus Langobardorum*, and was promulgated by King Rothari at a diet held at Pavia on 22 November 643. This work, composed at one time and arranged on a systematic plan, is very remarkable. The compilers knew Roman law, but drew upon it only for their method of presentation and for their terminology; and the document presents Germanic law in its purity. Rothar's edict was augmented by his successors: Grimwald (668) added nine chapters; Liutprand (713-735), fifteen volumes, containing a great number of ecclesiastical enactments; Ratchis (746), eight chapters; and Aistulf (755), thirteen chapters. After the union of the Lombards to the Frankish kingdom, the capitularies made for the entire kingdom were applicable to Italy. There were also special capitularies for Italy, called *Capitula Italica*, some of which were appended to the edict of Rothar.

At an early date, compilations were formed in Italy for the use of legal practitioners and jurists. Eberhard, duke and margrave of Rhaetia and Friuli, arranged the contents of the edict with its successive *additamenta* into a *Concordia de singulis causis* (829-832). In the 10th century a collection was made of the capitularies in use in Italy, and this was known as the *Capitulare Langobardorum*. Then appeared, under the influence of the school of law at Pavia, the *Liber legis Langobardorum*, also called *Liber Papiensis* (beginning of 11th century), and the *Lombarda* (end of 11th century), in two forms, that given in a Monte Cassino manuscript and known as the *Lombarda Casinensis* and the *Lombarda Vulgata*. In the *Liber Papiensis* each section of the edict is accompanied by specimen pleadings setting out the cause of action: in this way it comes near to being a treatment of substantive law as opposed to a simple tariff of penalties as found in the other *Leges barbarorum*

There are editions of the *Edictus*, the *Concordia*, and the *Liber Papiensis* by F. Bluhme and A. Boretius in the *Monumenta Germaniae Historica* series, Leges (in folio) vol. iv. Bluhme also gives the rubrics of the *Lombardae*, which were published by F. Lindenberg in his *Codex legum antiquarum* in 1613. For further information on the laws of the Lombards see J. Merkel, *Geschichte des Langobardenrechts* (1850); A. Boretius, *Die Kapitularien im Langobardenreich* (1864); and C. Kier, *Edictus Rotari* (Copenhagen, 1898). Cf. R. Dareste in the *Nouvelle Revue historique de droit français et étranger* (1900, p. 143).

Lombard law, as developed by the Italian jurists, was by far the most sophisticated of the early Germanic systems, and some (e.g. Frederick William Maitland) have seen striking similarities between it and early English law. It remained living law, subject to modifications, both in the Kingdom of the Lombards that became the Carolingian Kingdom of Italy and in the Duchy of Benevento that became the Kingdom of Naples and continued to play a role in the latter as late as the 18th century. The *Libri Feudorum*, explaining the distinctive Lombard version of feudalism, were frequently printed together with the Corpus Juris Civilis and were considered the academic standard for feudal law, influencing other countries including Scotland.

Lex Baiuvariorum

We possess an important law of the Bavarians, whose duchy was situated in the region east of the river Lech. Parts of this law have been taken directly from the Visigothic law of Euric and from the law of the Alamanni. The Bavarian law, therefore, is later than that of the Alamanni. It dates unquestionably from a period when the Frankish authority was very strong in Bavaria, when the dukes were subjects of the Frankish kings. The law's compilation is most commonly dated between 744 and 748, by the following argument; Immediately after the revolt of Bavaria in 743 the Bavarian Duke Odilo (died 748) was forced to submit to Pippin the Younger and Carloman, the sons of Charles Martel, and to recognize Frankish suzerainty. A little earlier, in 739, the church of Bavaria had been organized by St. Boniface, and the country divided into several bishoprics; and we find frequent references to these bishops (in the plural) in the law of the Bavarians. On the other hand, we know that the law is anterior to the reign of Duke Tassilo III (749-788). The date of compilation must, therefore, be placed between 744 and 748. Against this argument, however, it is very likely that Odilo recognized Frankish authority before 743; he took refuge at Charles Martel's court that year and married one of Martel's daughters. His "revolt" may have been in support of the claims of Pippin and Carloman's half-brother Grifo, not opposition to Frankish rule per se. Also, it is not clear that the Lex Baiuvariorum refers to multiple bishops in the duchy at the same time; when a bishop is accused of a crime, for instance, he is to be tried by the duke, and not by a council of fellow bishops as canon law required. So, it is possible that the Bavarian law was compiled earlier, perhaps between 735 (the year of Odilo's succession) and 739.

Lex Frisionum

The *Lex Frisionum* of the duchy of Frisia consists of a medley of documents of the most heterogeneous character. Some of its enactments are purely pagan, thus one paragraph allows the mother to kill her new-born child, and another prescribes the immolation to the gods of the defiler of their temple; others are purely Christian, such as those that prohibit incestuous marriages and working on Sunday. The law abounds in contradictions and repetitions, and the compositions are calculated in different moneys. From this it appears the documents were merely materials collected from various sources and possibly with a view to the compilation of a homogeneous law. These materials were apparently brought together at the beginning of the 9th century, at a time of intense legislative activity at the court of Charlemagne.

Lex Saxonum

The *Lex Saxonum* has come down to us in two manuscripts and two old editions (those of B. J. Herold and du Tillet), and the text has been edited by Karl von Richthofen in the *Mon. Germ. hist, Leges*, v. The law contains ancient customary enactments of Saxony, and, in the form in which it reached us, is later than the conquest of Saxony by Charlemagne. It is preceded by two capitularies of Charlemagne for Saxony, the *Capitulatio de partibus Saxoniae* (A. Boretius i. 68), which dates undoubtedly from 782, and is characterized by great severity, death being the penalty for every offence against the Christian religion; and the *Capitulare Saxonicum* (A. Boretius i. 71), of the 28 October 797, in which Charlemagne shows less brutality and pronounces simple compositions for misdeeds that formerly warranted death. The *Lex Saxonum* apparently dates from 803, since it contains provisions that are in the *Capitulare legi Ribuariae additum* of that year. The law established the ancient customs, at the same time eliminating anything that was contrary to the spirit of Christianity; it proclaimed the peace of the churches, whose possessions it guaranteed and whose right of asylum it recognized.

Lex Angliorum et Werinorum, hoc est, Thuringorum

In early times there dwelt in Thuringia, south of the river Unstrut, the Angli, who gave their name to the pagus Engili, and to the east, between the Saale and the Elster, the Warni (Werini, or Varini), whose name is seen in Werenofeld. In the 9th century, however, this region (then called Werenofeld) was occupied by the Suebi, and the Warni and Angli either coalesced with the Thuringi or sought an asylum in the north of what is now Germany. A collection of laws has come down to us bearing the name of these two peoples, the *Lex Angliorum et Werinorum, hoc est, Thuringorum*. This text is a collection of local customs arranged in the same order as the law of the Ripuarian Franks. Parts of it are based on the *Capitulare legi Ribuariae additum* of 803, and it seems to have been drawn up in the same conditions and circumstances as the law of the Saxons. There is an edition of this code by Karl von Richthofen in the *Mon. Germ, hist., Leges,* v. 103. The old opinion that this law originated in the southern Netherlands is entirely without foundation.

Source http://en.wikipedia.org/wiki/Early_Germanic_law

Edictum Rothari

Illumination of a manuscript of the Edict of Rothari

The **Edictum Rothari** (also *Edictus Rothari* or *Edictum Rotharis*) was the first written compilation of Lombard law, codified and promulgated 22 November 643 by King Rothari. The custom (*cawarfidae*) of the Lombards, according to Paul the Deacon, the Lombard historian, had been held in memory before this. Now it was promulgated in Latin, a very vulgar and coarse Latin, by the king with the advice and consent of his council and his army.

The Edict, in 388 chapters, was primitive in comparison to other Germanic legislation of the time. It was also comparatively late, for the Franks, Visigoths, and Anglo-Saxons had all compiled codices of law long before. Unlike the *Breviarium Alaricianum* of Alaric II, it was mostly Germanic tribal law dealing with wergelds, inheritance, and duels, not a code of Roman laws. Despite its Latin, it was not a Roman product. Unlike the near-contemporary *Forum Iudicum*, it was not influenced by Canon law. Its only dealings with ecclesiastic matters was a prohibition on violence in churches. The Edict gives military authority to the dukes and gives civil authority to a *schulthais* (or reeve) in the countryside and a *castaldus* (or gastald) in the city.

The Edict was written down by one Ansoald, not a bishop or lawyer, but a scribe of Lombard origin. It was affirmed by a *gairethinx* convened by Rothari in 643. The *gairethinx* was a gathering of the army who passed the law by clashing their spears on their shields in old Germanic fashion, a fitting passing for so Germanic a Latin code.

The Edict makes no references to public life, the governance of trade, the duties of a citizen; instead it is minutely concerned with compensations for wrongs, a feature familiar from the *wergeld* of Anglo-Saxons, and the defence of property rights. Though Lombard women were always in some status of wardship to the males of the family, and though a freeborn Lombard woman who married an *aldius* (half-free) or a slave might be slain or sold by her male kin, the respect, amounting to taboo, that was owed to a freeborn Lombard woman was notable: if any one should "place himself in the way" of a free woman or girl, or injure her, he must pay nine hundred solidi, an immense sum. For comparison, if any one should "place himself in the way" of a free man he must pay him twenty solidi— if he had not done him any bodily injury— and in similar cases involving another man's slave or handmaid or *aldius*, he must pay twenty solidi to the lord, the price for copulation with another man's slave. Roman slaves were of lower value in these matters than Germanic slaves "of the nations".

Physical injuries were all minutely catalogued, with a price for each tooth, finger or toe. Property was a concern: many laws dealt specially with injuries to an *aldius* or to a household slave. A still lower class, according to their assigned values, were the agricultural slaves.

In the laws of inheritance, illegitimate offspring had rights as well as legitimate ones. No father could disinherit his son except for certain grievous crimes. Donations of property were made in the presence of an assembly called the *thinc*, which gave rise to the barbarous Latin verb *thingare*, to grant or donate before witnesses. If a man shall wish to *thingare* his property, he must make the *gairethinx* ("spear donation") in the presence of free men.

Slaves might be emancipated in various ways, but there were severe laws for the pursuit and restoration of fugitives. In judicial procedure, a system of compurgation prevailed, as well as the wager of battle.

The general assembly of freemen continued to add ritual solemnity to important acts, such as the enactment of new laws or the selection of a king.

Lombard law governed Lombards solely, it must be remembered. The Roman population expected to live under long-codified Roman law. It was declared that foreigners who came to settle in Lombard territories were expected to live according to the laws of the Lombards, unless they obtained from the king the right to live according to some other law.

Later by the reign of King Liutprand (712-743) most inhabitants of Lombard Italy were considered "Lombards" regardless of remote ancestry and they followed Lombard Law.

Source http://en.wikipedia.org/wiki/Edictum_Rothari

Law of Hlothhere and Eadric

Law of Hlothhere and Eadric	
Ascribed to	Hloþhere (died 685) and Eadric (died 686), kings of Kent
Language	Old English
Date	7th century
Principal manuscript(s)	*Textus Roffensis*
First printed edition	George Hickes and Humfrey Wanley, *Linguarum Vett. Septentrionalium Thesaurus Grammatico-Criticus et Archaelogicus* (Oxford, 1703–5); see Law of Æthelberht#Manuscript, editions and translations
Genre	law code

The **Law of Hlothhere and Eadric** is an Anglo-Saxon legal text. It is attributed to the Kentish kings Hloþhere (died 685) and Eadric (died 686), and thus is believed to date to the second half of the 7th century. It is one of three extant early Kentish codes, along with the early 7th-century Law of Æthelberht and the early 8th-century Law of Wihtred. Written in language more modernised than these, the Law of Hlothhere and Eadric has more focus on legal procedure and has no religious content.

Provenance

The Law, as its name suggests, is attributed to the kings of Kent Hloþhere (died 685) and Eadric (died 686): this is stated in the rubric as well as the prologue of the main text. It is thought that the former reigned from 673 until 685, while Eadric ruled for a year and a half until his death in 686. The text does not indicate that Hloþhere and Eadric ruled together when it was issued, so it is possible that decrees of two reigns were brought together.

Like the other Kentish codes, the Law of Hloþhere and Eadric survives in only one manuscript, known as *Textus Roffensis* or the "Rochester Codex". This is a compilation of Anglo-Saxon historic and legal material drawn together in the early 1120s under Ernulf, bishop of Rochester. Hloþhere and Eadric's law occupies folios 3 to 5.

Despite being of similar date, the Old English of Hloþhere and Eadric's law is less archaic than the language of either the Law of Æthelberht (early 7th century) or the Law of Wihtred (early 8th century). The language appears to have been "updated" [Oliver] at a later date, and this may indicate that among the Kentish codes it went through a unique route of transmission, perhaps being more intensely consulted than the other two. It is possible too however that this is an accident of evidence, and that other similarly "updated" versions once existed for the other two codes: they simply were not the versions copied by the *Textus Roffensis* scribe.

Content

The content consists of a series of *domas*, "dooms" or judgments, and while providing historical information about Kentish compensation and management of public order, it focuses more on procedure than do the other two Kentish codes. There are eleven distinct groups of provisions according to the text's most recent editor Lisi Oliver, though F. L. Attenborough had previously broken it down into 15. Surprisingly, there are no provisions directly related to the church.

The provisions are ordered according to offence rather, as was the case in the Law of Æthelberht, according to social rank. The content of the law, by provision, is as follows:
1. Compensation for the killing of a noble by a servant
2. Compensation for the killing of a freeman by a servant
3. Accusations of person-stealing and compurgation for the accused
4. Provision for the family of dead freemen: maternal custody and the assignment of a male guardian from the paternal kin until a child reaches age 10
5. How to deal with stolen property and those possessing it
6. How to bring a charge: accusations, sureties and oaths

7–9. Fines for insults and disturbing the peace
10. Hospitality and responsibility for the behaviour of foreign guests
11. Acquisition of property in London (*Lundenwic*)

The law, particularly provision 6, is important to historians' understanding of the Anglo-Saxon arbitration process. A person, once accused, must take an oath promising to abide by the decision of a judge or accept a fine of 12 shillings. The accuser and accused must try to seek out an arbitrator acceptable to both. Once the judgment is delivered, the one ruled against must make good to the other, or swear on oath that he is innocent. If the accused refuses to cooperate, he is liable to a fine of 100 shillings—a freeman's wergild—and forbidden to swear his innocence in future.

It is also important for showing that the Kentish kingdom had control of London in the late 7th century. Provision 11 rules that Kentish men buying property in London must do so in public in the presence of two or three freemen of good standing or else before the king's *wicgerefan*, port-reeve. A predecessor of these kings, Eadbald son of Æthelberht (died 640), had issued a coin in London earlier in the 7th century.

Source http://en.wikipedia.org/wiki/Law_of_Hlothhere_and_Eadric

Law of Wihtred

Law of Wihtred	
Ascribed to	Wihtred, King of Kent
Language	Old English
Date	c. 695
Principal manuscript(s)	*Textus Roffensis*
First printed edition	George Hickes and Humfrey Wanley, *Linguarum Vett. Septentrionalium Thesaurus Grammatico-Criticus et Archaelogicus* (Oxford, 1703-5); see Law of Æthelberht#Manuscript, editions and translations
Genre	law code

The **Law of Wihtred** is an early English legal text attributed to the Kentish king Wihtred (died 725). It is believed to date to the final decade of the 7th century and is the last of three Kentish legal texts, following the Law of Æthelberht and the Law of Hlothhere and Eadric. It is devoted primarily to offences within and against the church, as well as church rights and theft.

Provenance

The prologue of the text and the red manuscript rubric attribute the law to Wihtred (died 725), king of Kent. Wihtred reigned from around or just after 690 to 725, and the text suggests he issued the law's provisions in 695.

Like the other Kentish codes, the Law of Hloþere and Eadric survives in only one manuscript, known as the "Rochester Codex" or *Textus Roffensis*. This is a compilation of Anglo-Saxon historic and legal material drawn together in the early 1120s under the supervision of Ernulf, bishop of Rochester. Wihtred's law occupies folios 5 to 6.

Issue

The prologue itself states that the "great men" of Kent issued the provisions before a large assembly of Kentish people, while Wihtred was "ruling in the fifth winter of his reign, in the ninth indiction, sixth day of *Rugern* [rye-harvest]" at "that place which is called Berghamstead" It is the only Kentish code to provide a regnal date, one working out to 6 September 695.

The prologue relates that Brihtwald, "archbishop of Britain" (*Bretone heahbiscop*, i.e., archbishop of Canterbury) was present, along with Gebmund, bishop of Rochester. This is appropriate as, unlike the two earlier Kentish codes, Wihtred's law is concerned with the church and religious matters. Similar to Ine's Law on several points, both laws may have drawn on Latin ecclesiastical canons.

Content

Recent editor of the text Lisi Oliver broke the provisions down as follows:

Provisions	Description
Prologue	Background and people behind the rulings
1–2	Rights of the Church
3–4	Provisions against sinful matrimony
5–6	Provisions against abusive ecclesiastics
7	Manumission (i.e., freeing of slaves)
8–11	Punishments for breaking church law
12–16	Exculpation (i.e., clearing oneself with an oath)
17–19	Church's right of exculpation
20–22	Punishment for theft

The chapter divisions are editorial and although divided into 22 chapters by Oliver, an earlier editor Frederick Attenborough had divided it into 28 separate chapters.

The Law allows that a bishop's word, like a king's, is to be regarded as legally incontrovertible without needing any concomitant oath, though lesser ecclesiastics must exculpate themselves before the altar. Provision 1 exempted the church of paying taxes to the king, but it also specified that churchmen must pray for and honour the king.

A charter of Wihtred's, dating c. 699, has an almost identical provision, exempting the kingdom's minsters from tax, but in turn requiring the king's position be respected otherwise. Some of the clauses regarding illicit marriages and the authority of bishops echo rulings made by the 672 Synod of Hereford, presided over by Theodore of Tarsus.

Included among the other religious offences punished are the consumption of meat during Christian fasting and gift-giving to pagan idols. The law also punishes nobles for working their slaves on Sabbath, and frees such slaves if they are so forced. Working on Sabbath was a concern also addressed in the near-contemporary Penitentials of Theodore [of Tarsus].

The theft provisions of the code allow the killing of thieves caught in the act, without the need to pay wergild. If the thief is not killed, the capturer is entitled to half the payment if the thief is subsequently ransomed, though the king may himself kill the thief or have him enslaved "across the sea" in addition to ransoming for the value of the thief's wergild. The law's final chapter provides that any foreigner or stranger who goes off the track and does not draw attention to himself by blowing his horn may be killed or captured.

Source http://en.wikipedia.org/wiki/Law_of_Wihtred

Law of Æthelberht

Law of Æthelberht

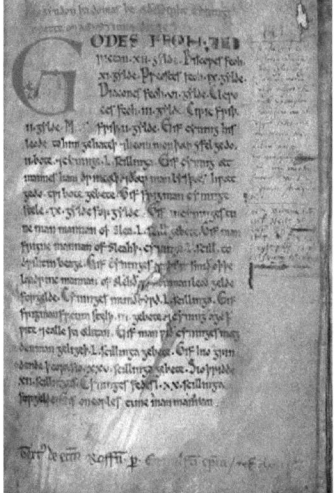

Opening folio of the code

Ascribed to	Æthelberht, king of Kent
Language	Old English
Date	7th century
Principal manuscript(s)	Textus Roffensis
First printed edition	George Hickes and Humfrey Wanley, *Linguarum Vett. Septentrionalium Thesaurus Grammatico-Criticus et Archaelogicus* (Oxford, 170
Genre	law code

The **Law of Æthelberht** is a set of legal provisions written in Old English, probably dating to the early 7th century. It originates in the kingdom of Kent, and is the first Germanic-language law code. It is also thought to be the earliest example of a document written in English, though extant only in an early 12th-century manuscript, *Textus Roffensis*.

The code is concerned primarily with preserving social harmony, through compensation and punishment for personal injury. Compensations are arranged according to social rank, descending from king to slave. The initial provisions of the code offer protection to the church. Though the latter were probably innovations, much of the remainder of the code may be derived from earlier legal custom transmitted orally.

Manuscript, editions and translations

There is only one surviving manuscript of Æthelberht's law, *Textus Roffensis* or the "Rochester Book". The Kentish laws occupy folios 1 to 6, of which Æthelberht's has 1 to 3. This is a compilation of Anglo-Saxon laws, lists and genealogies drawn together in the early 1120s, half a millennium after Æthelberht's law is thought to have been first written down. Æthelberht's law precedes the other Kentish law codes, which themselves precede various West Saxon and English royal legislation, as well as charters relating to Rochester Cathedral. Æthelberht's law is written in the same hand as the laws of other Kentish monarchs.

The compilation was produced at the instigation of Ernulf, bishop of Rochester, friend of the lawyer-bishop Ivo of Chartres. Ernulf was a legally minded bishop like Ivo, a canon lawyer and judge. He was responsible for commissioning copies of the *Anglo-Saxon Chronicle* at Canterbury Cathedral Priory and Peterborough Abbey, as prior and abbot respectively.

Francis Tate made a transcription of *Textus Roffensis* .c 1589, which survives as British Museum MS Cotton Julius CII. Henry Spelman, *Ecclesiarum Orbis Brittanici* (London, 1639), provided a Latin translation of provisions relating to the church. In 1640 Johannes de Laet translated the whole code into Latin. Though no original survives, several 18th century authors copied it. The first full edition (with Latin translation) was: George Hickes and Humfrey Wanley, *Linguarum Vett. Septentrionalium Thesaurus Grammatico-Criticus et Archaelogicus* (Oxford, 1703–05)

Many other Latin translations editions of the Kentish laws or *Textus Roffensis* followed in the 18th, 19th and 20th centuries, mostly from English and German editors. Notable examples include:

Felix Liebermann, *Die Gesetze der Angelsachsen* (Halle, 1897–1916), with German translation

Frederick Levi Attenborough, *The Laws of the Earliest English Kings* (Cambridge, 1922), with English translation

Lisi Oliver, *The Beginnings of English Law* (Toronto, 2002), with English translation

Origin

The code is attributed to Æthelberht, and for this reason is dated to that king's reign (c. 590 – 616x618). Æthelberht's code is thought to be both the earliest law code of any kind in any Germanic language and the earliest surviving document written down in the English language. Æthelberht is thought to be the king behind the code because the law's red-ink introductory rubric in *Textus Roffensis* attributes it to him.

Bede (*Historia Ecclesiastica* ii. 5), writing in Northumbria more than a century after King Æthelberht, attributes a code of laws to the king:

Among the other benefits which he thoughtfully conferred on his people, he also established enacted judgments for them, following the examples of the Romans, with the council of his wise men. These were written in English speech, and are held and observed by them to this day.

Bede goes on to describe details of the

code accurately. In the introduction to Alfred the Great's law the latter king relates that he consulted the laws of Æthelberht.

The code as it survives was not written in the king's name and the 12th-century author of the rubric may have been influenced by Bede in his attribution. The lack of attribution in the original text may be a sign that law-making was not primarily a royal activity as it was to become in later centuries.

There is evidence that much of the code was taken from pre-existing customary practice transmitted orally. The church provisions aside, the code's structure looks like an "architectural mnemonic", proceeding from top to bottom. It begins with the king and ends with slaves. Likewise, the section on personal injuries, which contains most of the code's provisions, begins with hair at the top of the body and ends with the toenail. Use of poetic devices such as consonance and alliteration also indicate the text's oral background. Æthelberht's law is hence largely derived from *ælþeaw*, established customary law, rather than royal *domas*, "judgements".

It is not clear why the code was written down however. The suggested date coincides with the coming of Christianity—the religion of the Romans and Franks—to the English of Kent. The code may be an attempt to imitate the Romans and establish the Kentish people as a respectable "civilised" people. Christianity and writing were furthered too by the Kentish king's marriage to Bertha, daughter of the Frankish king Charibert I. There have been suggestions that Augustine of Canterbury may have urged it. Legal historian Patrick Wormald argued that it followed a model from the 614 Frankish church council in Paris, which was attended by the abbot of St Augustine's and the bishop of Rochester. The wergeld ratios for churchmen in Æthelberht's code are similar to those of other Germanic laws, like *Lex Ribuaria* and the Swabian and Bavarian laws.

Content and language

Patrick Wormald divided the text into the following sections (the chapter numbers are those in Frederick Levi Attenborough's *Laws of the Earliest English Kings* and in Lisi Oliver's *Beginnings of English Law*):

Compensation for churchmen [Attenborough: 1 ; Lisi: 1–7]
Compensation for the king and his dependents [Attenborough: 2–12; Lisi: 8–17]
Compensation for an *eorl* and his dependents [Attenborough: 13–14; Lisi: 18–19]
Compensation for a *ceorl* and his dependents [Attenborough: 15–25, 27–32; Lisi: 20–26, 28–32]
Compensation for the semi-free [Attenborough: 26–27 Lisi: 26–27]
Personal injuries [Attenborough: 33–72; Lisi: 33–71]
Compensation and injuries concerning women [Attenborough: 73–84; Lisi: 72–77]
Compensation for servants [Attenborough: 85–88; Lisi: 78–81]
Compensation for slaves [Attenborough: 89–90; Lisi: 82–83]

Another legal historian, Lisi Oliver, offered a similar means of division:

Offences against the church and secular public assembly [Lisi: 1–7]
Offences relating to the king and his household [Lisi: 1–7]
Offences against *eorlas* ("noblemen") [Lisi: 8–17]
Offences against *ceorlas* ("freemen") [Lisi: 20–32]
Personal injury offences [Lisi: 33–71]
Offences against women [Lisi: 72–77]
Offences against *esnas* ("semi-free", "servants") [Lisi: 78–81]
Offences against *þeowas* ("slaves") [Lisi: 81–83]

In addition to protecting church property, the code offers a fixed means of making social conflict and its escalation less likely and ending feud by "righting wrongs" [Wormald]. Two units of currency are used, the *scilling* and the *sceatt*. In Æthelberht's day a *sceatt* was a unit of gold with the weight of a grain of barley, with 20 *sceattas* per *scilling*. One ox was probably valued at one *scilling* or "shilling".

The law is written in Old English, and there are many archaic features to the code's language. For instance, it uses an instrumental "dative of quantity" [Oliver] that is obsolete in later Old English grammar: *Gif friman edor gegangeð, iiii scillingum gebete* ("If a freeman enters an enclosure, let him pay with 4 shillings"). This is a construction found in other West Germanic languages but not elsewhere in Old English except once in the Laws of Hlothhere and Eadric (2.1). As another example, in the apodosis the verb is always in the end position in Æthelberht's law; while this is grammatical in Old English, it is an archaic construction for a legal text.

Words such as *mæthlfrith* ("assembly peace") *drihtinbeage* ("lord-payment"), *leodgeld* ("person-price"), *hlaf-ætan* ("loaf-eater"), *feaxfang* ("seizing of hair") and *mægðbot* ("maiden-compensation") are either absent in other Old English texts or very rare. Doubling vowels to indicate length (for instance, *taan*, "foot"), common to all written insular languages in the early Middle Ages but increasingly uncommon later on, occurs three times in Æthelberht's code but not elsewhere in *Textus Roffensis*.

Source http://en.wikipedia.org/wiki/Law_of_Æthelberht

Lex Alamannorum

The terms **Lex Alamannorum** and **Pactus Alamannorum** refer to two early medieval law codes of the Alamanni. They were first edited in parts in 1530 by Johannes Sichard in Basel.

Pactus Alamannorum

The *Pactus Alamannorum* or *Pactus*

legis Alamannorum is the older of the two codes, dating to the early 7th century. It is preserved in a single manuscript of the 9th to 10th century.

Lex Alamannorum

The *Lex Alamannorum* is preserved in some 50 manuscripts dating to between the 8th and 12th centuries. The text's first redaction is ascribed to the Alamannic duke Lantfrid in ca. 730. It is divided into clerical law, ducal law and popular law.

Chapter 3.1 treats church asylum: no fugitive seeking refuge in a church should be removed by force, or be killed within the church. Instead, the pursuers should assure the priest that the fugitive's guilt is forgiven. In 3.3, penalties for the violation of the asylum are set at 36 solidi to be paid to the church and an additional 40 solidi to be paid to the authorities for violation of the law.

Chapter 56.1 regulates penalties for violence towards women. If someone uncovers the head of a free, unmarried woman, he is fined with 6 solidi. If he lifts her dress so that her genitals or her buttocks become visible, he is fined with 12 solidi. If he rapes her, he is fined with 40 solidi. 56.2 doubles these penalties if the victim is a married woman.

Source http://en.wikipedia.org/wiki/Lex_Alamannorum

Lex Baiuvariorum

The **Lex Baiuvariorum** (also *Lex Baiuwariorum*, *Lex Bajuvariorum*, or *Lex Baivariorum*) was a collection of the tribal laws of the Bavarii of the sixth through eighth centuries. The first compilation was edited by Eberswind, first abbot of Niederaltaich, in 741 or 743. Duke Odilo, founder supplemented the code around 748. It is one of the most well documented bodies of Germanic tribal law.

Parts of the *Lex Baiuvariorum* are identical with the Visigothic Code of Euric and from the *Lex Alamannorum*. The Bavarian law, therefore, is later than that of the Alamanni. It dates unquestionably from a period when the Frankish authority was very strong in Bavaria, when the dukes were vassals of the Frankish kings. Immediately after the revolt of Bavaria in 743, the Bavarian Duke Odilo was forced to submit to Pippin the Younger and Carloman, the sons of Charles Martel, and to recognize the Frankish suzerainty. About the same period, too, the church of Bavaria was organized by St Boniface, and the country divided into several bishoprics; and we find frequent references to these bishops (in the plural) in the law of the Bavarians. On the other hand, we know that the law is anterior to the reign of Duke Tassilo III (749-788). The date of compilation must, therefore, be placed between 743 and 749.

Wilhelm Störmer claims that though the *Lex Baiuvariorum* uses some identical titles as Visigothic and Alamani texts, synodal texts and the Tradition Book of Freising indicate that it cannot simply be a copy. K. Reindels claims that the law could have been developed in stages, starting with the reign of Theudebert I (539–548) until we have the version that we know today created during the reign of Odillo. What is certain is that the *Lex Baiuvariorum* was created at the behest of the Frankish overlords.

The *Lex Baiuvariorum* consists mostly of individual acts the penalty in cash to be paid to the victim or the victim's family as well as the public treasury. Many of the extant manuscripts are in a small format, a clear indication that the lawbook was at hand when the lord held court. The text is written in Latin.

The *Lex Baiuvariorum* is divided into 23 titles. Titles 1–6 regulate the law of the different social ranks. Titles 7-23 offer legal rulings on criminal and private law.

Title I: Protection of the church, spiritual men, its people and property including servants and wards.
Title II: Protection of the duke, his office, and his military operations.
Title III: Stipulates the Agilolfings as the leading noble family from which the rulers of Bavaria are chosen. The other ruling families are: Huosi, Trozza, Fagana, Hahilinga, and Ariona.
Title IV: The protection of the free. Under *free*, the *Lex Baiuvariorum* makes a distinction between *those who are free* and *those who have been set free*. Fines for breaking the law varies depending on the status of the individuals involved: free, set free, and unfree.
Title VIII: On Women and their Legal Causes that often occur. First and foremost, addresses the fines and instances of justified homicide incidental to acts of female (free or bonded) infidelity and adulterous acts. Addresses, too, fines incurred by male (free or bonded) misconduct and molestation of women

The laws remained in effect until 1180. The oldest manuscript dates from around 800 and is in the possession of the library of the University of Munich.

Source http://en.wikipedia.org/wiki/Lex_Baiuvariorum

Lex Burgundionum

The *Lex Burgundionum* (**Burgundian Laws**, also *lex gundobada* or *loi gombette*) refers to the law code of the Burgundians, probably issued by king Gundobad. It is influenced by Roman law and deals with domestic laws concerning marriage and inheritance as well as regulating weregild and other penalties. Interaction between Burgundians is treated separately from interaction between Burgundians and Gallo-Romans. The oldest of the 14 surviving manuscripts of the text dates to the 9th century, but the code's institution is ascribed to king Gundobad (died 516), with a possible revision by his successor Sigismund (died 523). The *Lex Romana Burgundionum* is a separate code, containing various laws taken from Roman sources, probably intended to apply to the Burgundians' Gallo-Roman subjects. The oldest copy of this text dates to the 7th century.

Sigismund

The *Lex Burgundionum* code was compiled by King Gundobad (474-516), very probably after his defeat by Clovis I in 500. Some *additamenta* were subsequently introduced, either by Gundobad himself or by his son Sigismund. This law bears the title of *Liber Constitutionum*, indicating that it emanated from the king; it is also known as the *Lex Gundobada* or *Lex Gombata*. It was used for cases between Burgundians, and was also applicable to cases between Burgundians and Romans. For cases between Romans, however, Gundobald compiled the *Lex Romana Burgundionum*, called sometimes, through a misreading of the manuscript, the *Liber Papiani*, or simply *Papianus*.

Background

The Burgundian kingdom is one of the early Germanic kingdoms that existed within the Roman Empire. In the late fifth and early sixth centuries, the Burgundian kings Gundobad and Sigismund compiled and codified laws to govern the members of their Barbarian tribe, as well as Romans living amongst them. Those laws governing the Burgundians themselves are called collectively the *Lex Burgundionum*, while the laws governing the Romans are known collectively as the *Lex Romana Burgundionum*. Both are extant. The laws codified in the Burgundian Code reflect the earliest fusion of German tribal culture with the Roman system of government. It promoted and helped maintain harmonious relations between such widely different people who had been previous enemies. More devotion has been given to other Germanic tribes of this time and little is known about the culture and way of life of the Burgundians beyond what can be inferred from their legal code. Dr. Katherine Fischer Drew claims that it is the most influential of all barbarian law codes because of its survival, even after Frankish conquest, until the ninth century.

Once the Romans realized they could not stop the continual attacks by the invading Germanic tribes after nearly 200 years of fending them off, they created territorial agreements with them, including the Burgundians. These agreements are known as a system of *foederati*, which, among other factors, led to the ultimate demise of the western Roman Empire. Roman Emperor Honorius invited the Burgundians to join the Roman Empire with a capital at Worms through this concept of *foederati* – allies or federated peoples – in 406. The Burgundians were soon defeated by the Huns, but once again given land near Lake Geneva for Gundioc (r. 443-474) to establish a second federate kingdom within the Roman Empire in 443. This alliance was a contractual agreement between the two peoples. Gundioc's people were given one-third of Roman slaves and two-thirds of the land within Roman territory. The Burgundians were allowed to establish an independent federate kingdom within the Empire and received the nominal protection of Rome for their agreement to defend their territories from other outsiders. This contractual relationship between the guests, Burgundians, and hosts, Romans, supposedly provided legal and social equality. However, Drew argues that the property rights and social status of the guests may have given them disproportionate leverage over their hosts. More recently, Henry Sumner Maine argues that the Burgundians exercised "tribe-sovereignty" rather than complete territorial sovereignty.

Gundioc's son, Gundobad (r. 474-516), began commission for his kingdom's legal codification in 483, which his son and successor, Sigismund (r. 516-532) completed. The laws deal mostly with inheritance and monetary compensation for physical injury. The earlier work, *antiquae*, and the later additions, *novellae*, together make the whole Burgundian Code. The Franks began attacking the Burgundians in 523 and completely defeated them by 534, when Sigismund's brother, Godomar (r. 532-534), fled and left the kingdom to be divided amongst Frankish rulers. However, the Franks kept Burgundian law in practice.

Contents of the *Lex*

The Burgundian Code consists of two sets of laws, the earlier Book of Constitutions or Law of Gundobad, or *Liber Constitutionum sive Lex Gundobada*, and Additional Enactments, or *Constitutiones Extravagantes*. The laws of both parts are intended to govern the personal relations between individuals. The Law of Gundobad (Titles II-XLI) is a compilation of existing customary laws. These laws are mostly a codification of customs that had been accepted as law throughout the tribe through common practice. Drew describes Gundobad's work "as a recording of the customs of his people issued with the consent of the people". The later additions (Titles LXXXVIII-CV and *Constitutiones Extravagantes*), which are believed to have been issued primarily by Sigismund, are more rhetorical. They begin with general legal principles and dictate from the judgment of the king how a disputed situation may be handled.

It is this conflict between customary and statutory law that one sees the blending of Burgundian and Roman laws. Roman influence is apparent in the very act of writing down Germanic customary law. According to Edward Peters in his foreword to Drew's translation of the Burgundian Code, Roman ideals triumphed when King Gundobad began organizing his people's customary laws in order for their codification. King Gundobad's singular action to codify laws can also be seen as a major change in Germanic culture as reflecting the emergence of the king as supreme judge and lawmaker. The Burgundians already had traditions and laws for arbitrating disputes among its people, but Romans brought with them organizational structure for a more legitimate government.

A great number of laws deal specifically with Germanic-style monetary retribution for intentional physical harm on one another. Punitive fines, rather than further physical injury or capital punishment, were used to regulate physical injury to prevent blood feud between two members of a tribal kinship.

Along with money payments in compensation for physical injuries, the Burgundian Code also incorporates the wergeld, another Germanic institution. Drew defines wergelds as "the sum at which a man was valued and by the payment of which his death could be compensated". The wergeld of the upper class of freemen was worth a payment of 300 solidi, the underclass freeman worth 200 solidi, and the lowest class of freeman was 150 solidi. Drew believes that the family was the absolute most important social institution in Germanic tribes.

Additionally, its inheritance laws were based on Germanic custom. Land was passed down through a strict law of familial succession, which differs greatly from Roman laws on property that allow property to be acquired through ways other than hereditary inheritance, such as buying and selling or testimonial succession. Among other features, a widow was entitled to a life interest in a third of her husband's landed property: this may have been the prototype of the analogous institution of dower in early English law.

The laws of the Burgundians show strong traces of Roman influence. It recognizes the will and attaches great importance to written deeds, but on the other hand, sanctions the judicial duel and the cojuratores (sworn witnesses). The vehement protest made in the 9th century by Agobard, bishop of Lyon, against the *Lex Gundobada* shows that it was still in use at that period. So late as the 10th and even the 11th centuries we find the law of the Burgundians invoked as personal law in Cluny charters, but doubtless these passages refer to accretions of local customs, rather than to actual paragraphs of the ancient code.

Source http://en.wikipedia.org/wiki/Lex_Burgundionum

Lex Frisionum

Lex Frisionum, the "Law Code of the Frisians", was recorded in Latin during the reign of Charlemagne, after the year 785, when the Frankish conquest of Frisia was completed by the final defeat of the Frisian king Radboud. The law code covered the region of the Frisians. The Frisians were divided into four legal classes, to whom the law, or those transgressions of it that incurred set fines, applied. They were the nobles, the freemen, the serfs and slaves. The clergy are not mentioned in the *Lex Frisionum* as they were not liable to civil law.

The Frisians received the title of freemen and were allowed to choose their own podestat or imperial governor. In the *Lex Frisionum* three districts of Frisia are clearly distinguished: the law governs all of Frisia, but West Frisia "between Zwin and Vlie" and East Frisia "between Lauwers and Weser" have certain stated exceptional provisions

At the partition treaty of Verdun (843) the whole of Frisia became part of Lotharingia; at the treaty of Meersen (870) it was briefly divided between the kingdoms of the East Franks (Austrasia) and the West Franks (Neustria), but in 808 the whole country was united to Austrasia.

The first twenty-two chapters of the Lex Frisionum are entirely concerned with schedules of fines (*compositio*) and wergeld, the compensations due victims or their kin, scheduled according to the social ranks of perpetrator and victim. Remarkably, the fine for killing a woman was exactly the same as for a man of the same rank, a feature of Frisian law that links it to Anglo-Saxon law, and stands apart from all other German codes. A further eleven chapters contain the 'Additions of the Wise Men' (*Additio sapientum*), ten subheadings from the judgements of **Wiemar** and of **Saxmund** of whom nothing is known, as well as sections from the *Lex Thuringorum* ("Law Code of the Thuringians") to cover instances not previously covered.

A noble's defense was to gather a specified number of "oath-helpers" willing to swear that the crime was not committed.

The only trial by ordeal mentioned (twice) in the Lex Frisionum is the ordeal by boiling water. A stone had to be withdrawn from a seething cauldron: if the blisters were healed within three days, the man was innocent.

Transmission

On numismatic ground based on the of fines (compositio) and wergeld, the laws from the Lex Frisionum date from the first half of the 7th century at the latest.

There are no surviving manuscripts of the Lex Frisionum. The only testimony is the oldest printed version, which dates from 1557. In that year, the printer Joannis Basilius Herold from Basel made a compilation of all Germanic laws from the time of Charlemagne, *Originum ac Germanicarum Antiquitatum Libri....* Among them he printed the Lex Frisionum, but from what source, or how corrupt his text, is unknown.

The surviving version is apparently a rough draft, still retaining pagan elements, which doubtless would have been edited out in the finished version, which Charlemagne apparently contemplated assembling for each of the Germanic peoples in his empire.

Source http://en.wikipedia.org/wiki/Lex_Frisionum

Lex Ripuaria

The ***Lex Ripuaria*** is a 7th century collection of Germanic law, the laws of the Ripuarian Franks. It is a major influence on the *Lex Saxonum* of AD 802. The *Lex Ripuaria* originated about 630 around Cologne and has been described as a later development of the Frankish laws known from *Lex Salica*.

The 35 surviving manuscripts, as well as those now lost which served as the basis of the old editions, do not go back beyond the time of Charlemagne. In all these MSS. the text is identical, but it is a revised text - in other words, we have only a *lex emendata*. On analysis, the law of the Ripuarians, which contains 89 chapters, falls into three heterogeneous divisions. Chapters 1-31 consist of a scale of compositions; but, although the fines are calculated, not on the unit of 15 *solidi*, as in the Salic Law, but on that of 18 *solidi*, it is clear that this part is already influenced by the Salic Law. Chapters 32-64 are taken directly from the Salic Law; the provisions follow the same arrangement; the unit of the compositions is 15 *solidi*; but capitularies are interpolated relating to the affranchisement and sale of immovable property. Chapters 65-89 consist of provisions of various kinds, some taken from lost capitularies and from the Salic Law, and others of unknown origin.

The compilation apparently goes back to the reign of Dagobert I (629-639), to a time when the power of the mayors of the palace was still minimal, since we read of a mayor being threatened with the death penalty for taking bribes in the course of his judicial duties. It is probable, however, that the first two parts are older than the third. Already in the Ripuarian Law the divergences from the old Germanic law are greater than in the Salic Law. In the Ripuarian Law a certain importance attaches to written deeds; the clergy are protected by a higher wergild: 600 *solidi* for a priest, and 900 for a bishop; on the other hand, more space is given to the *cojuratores* (sworn witnesses); and the appearance of the judicial duel is noted, which is not mentioned in the Salic Law.

Editions

R. Sohm, "Monumenta Germaniae", Leges V (1883)
Source http://en.wikipedia.org/wiki/Lex_Ripuaria

Lex Saxonum

The **Lex Saxonum** are a series of laws issued by Charlemagne in 785 as part of his plan to subdue the Saxon nation. The law is thus a compromise between the traditional customs and statutes of the pagan Saxons and the established laws of the Frankish Empire.

The *Lex Saxonum* has come down to us in two manuscripts and two old editions (those of B. J. Herold and du Tillet), and the text has been edited by Karl von Richthofen in the *Mon. Germ. hist., Leges*, v. The law contains ancient customary enactments of Saxony, and, in the form in which it has reached us, is later than the conquest of Saxony by Charlemagne. It is preceded by two capitularies of Charlemagne for Saxony, the *Capitulatio de partibus Saxoniae* (A. Boretius i. 68), which dates undoubtedly from 782, and is characterized by great severity, death being the penalty for every offence against the Christian religion; and the *Capitulare Saxonicum* (A. Boretius i. 71), of the 28 October 797, in which Charlemagne shows less brutality and pronounces simple compositions for misdeeds which formerly entailed death. The *Lex Saxonum* apparently dates from 803, since it contains provisions which are in the *Capitulare legi Ribuariae additum* of that year. The law established the ancient customs, at the same time eliminating anything that was contrary to the spirit of Christianity; it proclaimed the peace of the churches, whose possessions it guaranteed and whose right of asylum it recognized.

Navigation menu

Personal tools
Create account
Log in

Namespaces
Article
Talk

Variants

Actions

Search

Navigation
Main page
Contents
Featured content
Current events
Random article
Donate to Wikipedia

Interaction
Help
About Wikipedia
Community portal
Recent changes
Contact Wikipedia

Toolbox
What links here
Related changes
Upload file
Special pages
Permanent link
Page information
Cite this page

Norwegian Code

Christian V of Denmark and Norway

The **Norwegian Code** (Norwegian: *Norske Lov*, abbreviated NL) is the oldest part of the Norwegian law still in force, partially in force in Norway, Iceland, and the Faroe Islands. It was given by Christian V of (Denmark and) Norway on 15 April 1687 and entered into force on 29 September 1688, as the legal code for the Kingdom of Norway including its dependencies (the Faroe Island, Iceland, and Greenland). Norway was a nominally sovereign kingdom, but politically (although not economically) the weaker part in a personal union with Denmark at the time. The Norwegian Code was largely based on the Danish Code (*Danske Lov*, DL), promulgated in 1683 and itself mostly based on older Danish laws, but the Norwegian Code had some differences from the Danish Code in some areas, such as inheritance law, agricultural law, law relating to hunting, fisheries and trade, and military issues. In the 19th and 20th centuries, most of the provisions were gradually repealed as they were replaced by modern laws. The code as such remains in force, and it was last amended on 1 January 1993. As late as the postwar era, the Supreme Courts of Denmark and Norway interestingly interpreted identical provisions from the Danish and Norwegian Code respectively; they came to the opposite conclusions regarding the meaning of identical provisions NL 6-10-2 (in force in Norway until 1985) and DL 6-10-2 (still in force in Denmark). The provision is ambiguously worded and regulates compensation for damage caused by livestock and dogs. The Supreme Court of Norway ruled on the meaning of this provision in 1954.

Norway's new Criminal Code entered into force in 1842, but crimes committed before that year were punished under the Norwegian Code. The Norwegian Code was last applied in a criminal case in August 1862, when 80 year old Lorentse Thomasdatter Vaagen admitted to having robbed and killed her friend Gunnil Heggelund in Trondhjem in 1827. She was sentenced to death, but the sentence was commuted to life imprisonment, and she died in the same year.

Parts of the Norwegian Code also remain in force in the former Norwegian dependencies Iceland and the Faroe Islands, which became part of Denmark with the dissolution of the Dano-Norwegian union in 1814. Iceland is today a sovereign state, while the Faroe Islands is a self-governing Danish dependency.

Background

It is also referred to as Christian V's Norwegian Code, to distinguish it from its predecessor, Christian IV's Norwegian Code, in force from 1604 to 1688. Christian IV's Norwegian Code was largely a translation into Danish of Magnus VI's Norwegian Code, promulgated in 1274 as a unified code of laws to apply for the whole country, including the Faroe Islands and Shetland, and replacing earlier regional laws.

Source http://en.wikipedia.org/wiki/Norwegian_Code

Raffelstetten Customs Regulations

Raffelstetten Customs Regulations (Latin: *Inquisitio de theloneis Raffelstettensis*, literally: "Inquisition on the Raffelstetten Tolls"), is the only legal document regulating customs in Early Medieval Europe. The inquiry was edited in the Monumenta Germaniae Historica (ed. A. Boretius and V. Krause, MGH Capit. 2, no. 253).

The document takes its name from Raffelstetten, a toll-bar on the Danube, a few kilometers downstream from Linz (it is now part of the town of Asten in Austria). There, the Carolingian king Louis the Child promulgated a regulation of toll-bars on his domains, after an inquiry dated between 903 and 906.

The customs regulations are priceless for documenting trade in Eastern Europe of the 9th and 10th centuries. The document makes it clear that Raffelstetten was a place where German slave traders and their Slavic counterparts exchanged goods. The Czech and Rus merchants sold wax, slaves, and horses to German merchants. Salt, weapons, and ornaments were sought by slave trading adventurers.

Perhaps the most striking feature of the regulations is the absence of Charlemagne's denarius, the only coin officially recognized in the Frankish Empire. Instead, the document mentions "skoti", a currency otherwise not attested in Carolingian Europe. It appears that both the name and weight of the "skoti" were borrowed from the Rus.

Vasily Vasilievsky notes that the document, being the first legal act to regulate the trade of the Rus', capped off a long tradition of trade between Germany and Kievan Rus. Alexander Nazarenko suggests that the trade route between Kiev and Regensburg (*strata legitima*, as it is labeled in the text) was as important in the period as that between Novgorod and Constantinople would be in the tenth century.

Source http://en.wikipedia.org/wiki/Raffelstetten_Customs_Regulations

Sachsenspiegel

The *Sachsenspiegel* (lit. "Mirror of the Saxons"; Low German: *Sassenspegel*, Middle Low German: *Sassen Speyghel*) is the most important law book and legal code of the German Middle Ages. Written ca. 1220 as a record of existing law, it was used in parts of Germany until as late as 1900, and is important not only for its lasting effect on German law, but also as an early example of written prose in a German language, being the first large legal document to have been written in (Middle Low) German, instead of Latin. A Latin edition is known to have existed, but only fragmented chapters remain.

History

The *Sachsenspiegel* was one of the first prose works in Low German (Middle Saxon) language. The original title is *Sassen Speyghel*, *Sachsenspiegel* being a later German translation. It is believed to have been compiled and translated from Latin by the Saxon administrator Eike von Repgow at the behest of his liege lord Graf Hoyer von Falkenstein in the years 1220 to 1235. Where the original was compiled is unclear. It was thought to have been written at Burg Falkenstein, but Peter Landau, an expert in medieval canon law recently suggested that it may have been written at the monastery of Altzelle (now Altzella).

The *Sachsenspiegel* served as a model for law books in German (Middle High German) like the *Augsburger Sachsenspiegel*, the *Deutschenspiegel*, and the *Schwabenspiegel*. Its influence extended into Eastern Europe, the Netherlands, and the Baltic States.

In Prussia, the *Sachsenspiegel* was used until the introduction of the *Allgemeines Landrecht für die preußischen Staaten* in 1794. In Saxony it was used

Choosing the king. Top: the three ecclesiastical princes choosing the king, pointing at him. Centre: the Count Palatine of the Rhine hands over a golden key, acting as a servant. Behind him, the Duke of Saxony with his marshall's staff and the Margrave of Brandenburg bringing a bowl of warm water, as a valet. Below, the new king in front of the great men of the empire (Heidelberg *Sachsenspiegel*, around 1300)

until the introduction of the Saxon Civil Code in 1865. In Anhalt and Thuringia the *Sachsenspiegel* was not replaced until the introduction of the German civil code, the *Bürgerliches Gesetzbuch* in 1900. Its precedents continued to be cited as recently as 1932 by the *Reichsgericht* (Supreme Court of the Reich) (RGZ 137, 373).

The influence of the *Sachsenspiegel*, or at least parallels with it, can still be found in modern German law, for instance in inheritance law and the law governing disputes between neighbors.

Branches of Law

The *Sachsenspiegel* contains two branches of law: common law and feudal law.

Common Law

The common law, or *Landrecht*, was the law of free people including farmers (known as "legal persons"). It contains important regulations concerning property rights, inheritances, matrimonies, the distribution of goods and the regulation of various legal disputes (e.g. between neighbors). It also regulates the criminal law and the constitution of the courts. In terms of modern legal systems it can be thought of as including criminal and civil law.

Feudal Law

The feudal law, or *Lehnrecht*, determined the relationship between different states and rulers, for example the election of emperors and kings, feudal rights, etc. Though it has no modern equivalent, it can be compared to what one would call today constitutional law.

The Sachsenspiegel acquired special significance through its exposition of the seven *Heerschilde* or "shields of knighthood":

King
Ecclesiastical princes
Lay princes
Free lords (*freie Herren*)
Schöffenbarfreie, vassals of free lords, ministeriales
Vassals of *Schöffenbarfreie* etc.
Unnamed.

Farmers and town burghers were not mentioned.

Extant copies

Four (of the original seven) illuminated manuscripts copies are still extant. They

20 • Salic law

Eike von Repgow from the *Oldenburg Sachsenspiegel*

are named after their present locations: Heidelberg, Oldenburg, Dresden, and Wolfenbüttel, and date from about 1300 to 1370.

Proverbs

Some German proverbs date from the Sachsenspiegel:
"Wer zuerst kommt, mahlt zuerst" (First come, first served, literally: "Who comes first, grinds first"), which is a rule for the order for grinding of corn by a miller.
"Wo der Esel sich wälzt, da muss er Haare lassen.", lit: "Where the donkey rolls, there it sheds hair." This is a rule for the jurisdiction of courts.
Source http://en.wikipedia.org/wiki/Sachsenspiegel

Salic law

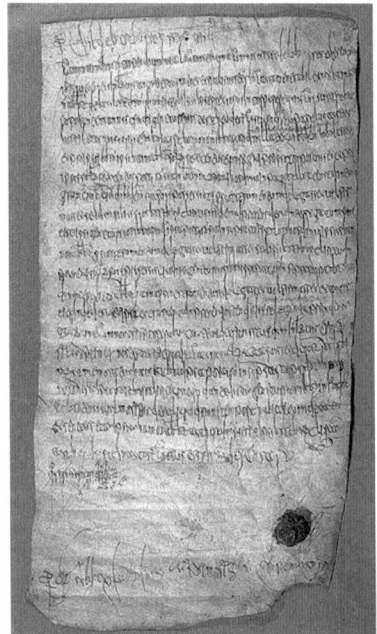

Record of a judgement by Childebert III

Salic law (/ˈsælɨk/ or /ˈseɪlɨk/; Latin: *Lex Salica*), or **Salian Law**, was the major body of Frankish law governing all the Franks of Frankia under the rule of its kings during the Old Frankish Period, approximately equal to the early Middle Ages. The laws were maintained in written form in the Latin language by a committee empowered by the monarch. Dozens of manuscripts dated from the 8th century of a putative original recension in the 6th century and three emendations as late as the 9th century have survived.

Salic law provided written codification of both civil law, such as the statutes governing inheritance, and criminal law, such as the punishment for murder. It has had a formative influence on the tradition of statute law that has extended to modern times in Central Europe, especially in the German states, France, Belgium, the Netherlands, parts of Italy, Austria and Hungary, Romania, and the Balkans.

History of the law

The original edition of the code was commissioned by the first king of all the Franks, Clovis I (c. 466–511), earlier than its publication date sometime between 507 and 511. He appointed four commissioners to research uses of laws that, until the publication of the *Salic Law*, were recorded only in the minds of designated elders, who would meet in council when their knowledge was re-

King Clovis dictates the *Salic Law* surrounded by his military chiefs.

quired. Transmission was entirely oral. Salic Law therefore reflects ancient usages and practices. In order to govern properly, the monarchs and their administrations needed the code in writing. The name of the code comes from the circumstance that Clovis was a Merovingian king ruling only the Salian Franks before his unification of Frankia. The law must have applied to the Ripuarian Franks as well; however, containing only 65 titles, it may not have included any special Ripuarian laws.

For the next 300 years the code was copied by hand and was amended as required to add newly enacted laws, revise laws that had been amended, and delete laws that had been repealed. In contrast to printing, hand copying is an individual act by an individual copyist with ideas and a style of his own. Each of the several dozen surviving manuscripts features a unique set of errors, corrections, content and organization. The laws are called "titles" as each one has its own name, generally preceded by *de*, "concerning." Different sections of titles acquired individual names revealing something about their provenances. Some of these dozens of names have been adopted for specific reference, often given the same designation as the overall work, *lex*.

Merovingian phase

The recension of Hendrik Kern organizes all of the manuscripts into five families according to similarity and relative chronological sequence, judged by content and dateable material in the text. Family I is the oldest, containing four manuscripts dated to the 8th and 9th centuries but containing 65 titles believed to be copies of originals published in the 6th century. In addition they feature the *Malbergse Glossen*, "Malberg Glosses," marginal glosses stating the native court word for some Latin words. These are named from native *malbergo*, "language of the court." Kern's Family II, represented by two manuscripts, is the same as Family I, except it contains "interpolations or numerous additions which point to a later period."

Carolingian phase

Family III is split into two divisions. The first, comprising three manuscripts, dated to the 8th-9th centuries, presents an expanded text of 99 or 100 titles. The Malberg Glosses are retained. The second, four manuscripts, not only drops the glosses, but "bears traces of attempts to make the language more concise." A statement gives the provenance: "in the 13th year of the reign of our most glorious king of the Franks, Pipin." Some of the internal documents were composed after the reign of Pepin the Short, but it is considered to be an emendation initiated by Pepin, and is therefore termed the *Pipina Recensio*.

Family IV also has two divisions, the first comprising 33 manuscripts; the second, one manuscript. They are characterized by the internal assignment of Latin names to various sections of different provenience. Two of the sections are dated to 768 and 778, but the emendation is believed to be dated to 798, late in the reign of Charlemagne. This edition calls itself the *Lex Salica Emendata* or the *Lex Reformata* or the *Lex Emendata*, and is clearly the result of a law code reform by Charlemagne.

By that time his Holy Roman Empire comprised most of Western Europe. He adds laws of choice taken from the earlier law codes of Germanics not originally part of Frankia. These are numbered into the laws that were there, but they have their own, quasi-sectional, title. All the Franks of Frankia were of course subject to the same law code, which retained the overall title of *Lex Salica*. These integrated sections borrowed from other Germanic codes are the *Lex Ribuariorum*, later *Lex Ribuaria*, laws adopted from the Ripuarian Franks, who, before Clovis, had been independent. The *Lex Alamannorum* took laws from the Alamanni, then subject to the Franks. Under the latter, they were governed by Frankish law, not their own. The inclusion of some of their law as part of the Salic Law must have served as a palliative. Charlemagne goes back even earlier to the *Lex Suauorum*, the ancient code of the Suebi preceding the Alemanni.

The language question

The Salic law code contains the earliest surviving attestations of Old Dutch. They consist mainly of stray words or glosses (*Malbergse glossen*), but include a full sentence:

Old Dutch	maltho	thi afrio	-	lito
Dutch	ik meld,	jou bevrijd ik,	-	laat
English	I declare,	- I free	you,	villein

A villein was a form of serfdom in the feudal system. He was a half-freed farmer; connected to the land of his lord he worked for, but not owned by his lord. In contrast, a serf was in full ownership of the lord.

Some tenets of the law

These laws and their interpretations grant insight to Frankish society. The criminal laws established damages to be paid and fines levied in recompense of injuries to persons and damage to goods, e.g., slaves, theft, and unprovoked insults. One-third of the fine paid court costs. Judicial interpretation was by a jury of peers.

The civil law establishes that an individual person is legally unprotected if he or she does not belong to a family. The rights of family members were defined; for example, the equal division of land among all living male heirs in opposition to primogeniture.

Agnatic succession

One tenet of the civil law is agnatic succession, the rule excluding females from the inheritance of a throne or fief. Indeed, "Salic law" has often been used simply as a synonym for agnatic succession. But the importance of Salic law extends beyond the rules of inheritance, as it is a direct ancestor of the systems of law in many parts of Europe today.

Salic law regulates succession according to sex. *Agnatic succession* means succession to the throne or fief going to an agnate of the predecessor; for example, a brother, a son, or nearest male relative through the male line, including collateral agnate branches, for example very distant cousins. Chief forms are *agnatic seniority* and *agnatic primogeniture*. The latter, which has been the most usual, means succession going to the eldest son of the monarch; if the monarch had no sons, the throne would pass to the nearest male relative in the male line.

Female inheritance

Concerning the inheritance of land, Salic Law said

But of Salic land no portion of the inheritance shall come to a woman: but the whole inheritance of the land shall come to the male sex.

or, another transcript:

concerning terra Salica no portion or inheritance is for a woman but all the land belongs to members of the male sex who are brothers.

As actually interpreted by the Salian Franks, the law simply prohibited women from inheriting, not all property (such as movables), but ancestral "Salic land"; and under Chilperic I sometime around the year 570, the law was actually amended to permit inheritance of land by a daughter if a man had no surviving sons. (This amendment, depending on how it is applied and interpreted, offers the basis for either Semi-Salic succession or male-preferred primogeniture, or both).

The wording of the law, as well as common usages in those days and centuries afterwards, seems to support an interpretation that inheritance is divided between brothers. And, if it is intended to govern succession, it can be interpreted to mandate agnatic seniority, not a direct primogeniture.

In its use by hereditary monarchies since the 15th century, aiming at agnatic succession, the Salic law is regarded as excluding all females from the succession as well as prohibiting succession rights to transfer through any woman. At least two systems of hereditary succession are direct and full applications of the Salic Law: agnatic seniority and agnatic primogeniture.

The so-called *Semi-Salic* version of succession order stipulates that firstly all male descendance is applied, including all collateral male lines; but if all agnates become extinct, then the closest heiress (such as a daughter) of the last male holder of the property inherits, and after her, her own male heirs according to the Salic order. In other words, the female closest to the last incumbent is regarded as a male for the purposes of inheritance/succession. This is a pragmatic way of putting order: the female is the closest, thus continuing the most recent incumbent's blood, and not involving any more distant relative than necessary (see, for example: Pragmatic Sanction of 1713 in Austria). At that order, the original primogeniture is not followed with regard to the requisite female. She could be a child of a relatively junior branch of the whole dynasty, but still inherits thanks to the longevity of her own branch.

From the Middle Ages, we have one practical system of succession in cognatic male primogeniture, which actually fulfills apparent stipulations of original Salic law: succession is allowed also through female lines, but excludes the females themselves in favour of their sons. For example, a grandfather, without sons, is succeeded by his grandson, a son of his daughter, when the daughter in question is still alive. Or an uncle, without his own children, is succeeded by his nephew, a son of his sister, when the sister in question is still alive.

Strictly seen, this fulfills the Salic condition of "no land comes to a woman, but the land comes to the male sex". This can be called a *Quasi-Salic* system of succession and it should be classified as primogenitural, cognatic, and male.

Applications of the law

In France

In 1316, King John I the Posthumous died, and for the first time in the history of the House of Capet, a king's closest living relative upon his death was not his son. French lords (notably led by the late king's uncle, Philip of Poitiers, the beneficiary of their position) wanted to forbid inheritance by a woman. These lords wanted to favour Philip's claim over John's half-sister Joan (later Joan II of Navarre), but disqualify her future claim to the French throne, and any possible future claims of Edward III of England. These events later led to the Hundred Years' War (1337–1453).

In 1328, a further limitation was needed, to bar inheritance by a male through a female line. A number of excuses were given for these applications of succession, such as "genealogical proximity with the king Saint Louis"; the role of monarch as war leader; and barring the realm going to an alien man and his clan through a woman, which also denied an order of succession where an alien man could become king of France by marriage to its queen, without necessarily having any French blood himself. Also, in 1316 the rival heir was a five-year-old female and powerless compared with the rival. In 1328, the rival was the king of England, against which France had been in a state of intermittent war for over 200 years. As far as can be ascertained, *Salic law* was not explicitly mentioned.

Jurists later resurrected the long-defunct Salic law and reinterpreted it to justify the line of succession arrived at in the cases of 1316 and 1328 by forbidding not only inheritance by a woman but also inheritance through a female line (*In terram Salicam mulieres ne succedant*).

Notwithstanding Salic law, when Francis II of Brittany died in 1488 without male issue, his daughter Anne succeeded him and ruled as duchess of Brittany until her death in 1514. (Brittany had been inherited by women earlier – Francis's own dynasty obtained the duchy through their ancestress Duchess Constance of Brittany in the 12th century.) Francis's own family, the Montfort branch of the ducal house, had obtained Brittany in the 1350s on the basis of agnatic succession, and at that time, their succession was limited to the male line only.

This law was by no means intended to cover all matters of inheritance — for example, not the inheritance of movables – only those lands considered "Salic" — and there is still debate as to the legal definition of this word, although it is generally accepted to refer to lands in the royal fisc. Only several hundred years later, under the Direct Capetian kings of France and their English contemporaries who held lands in France, did Salic law become a rationale for enforcing or debating succession. By then somewhat anachronistic (there were no Salic lands, since the Salian monarchy and its lands had originally emerged in what is now the Netherlands), the idea was resurrected by Philip V in 1316 to support his claim to the throne by removing his niece Jeanne from the succession, following the death of his nephew John.

In 1328, at latest, the Salic Law needed a further interpretation to forbid not only inheritance by a woman, but inheritance through a female line, in order to bar the male Edward III of England, descendant of French kings through his mother Isabel of France, from the succession. When the Direct Capetian line ended, the law was contested by England, providing a putative motive for the Hundred Years' War.

Shakespeare claims that Charles VI rejected Henry V's claim to the French throne on the basis of Salic law's inheritance rules, leading to the Battle of Agincourt. In fact, the conflict between Salic law and English law was a justification for many overlapping claims between the French and English monarchs over the French Throne.

Other European applications

A number of military conflicts in European history have stemmed from the application of, or disregard for, Salic law. The Carlist Wars occurred in Spain over the question of whether the heir to the throne should be a female or a male relative. The War of the Austrian Succession was triggered by the Pragmatic Sanction in which Charles VI of Austria, who himself had inherited the Austrian patrimony over his nieces as a result of Salic law, attempted to ensure the inheritance directly to his own daughter Maria Theresa of Austria, this being an example of an operation of the *Semi-Salic law*.

In the modern kingdom of Italy under the house of Savoy the succession to the throne was regulated by Salic law.

The British and Hanoverian thrones separated after the death of King William IV of the United Kingdom and of Hanover in 1837. Hanover practised the Salic law, while Britain did not. King William's niece Victoria ascended to the throne of Great Britain and Ireland, but the throne of Hanover went to William's brother Ernest, Duke of Cumberland. Salic law was also an important issue in the Schleswig-Holstein question, and played a weary prosaic day-to-day role in the inheritance and marriage decisions of common princedoms of the German states such as Saxe-Weimar, to cite a representative example. It is not much of an overstatement to say that European nobility confronted Salic issues at every turn and nuance of diplomacy, and certainly, especially when negotiating marriages, for the entire male line had to be extinguished for a land title to pass (by marriage) *to a female's husband*—women rulers were anathema in the German states well into the modern era.

In a similar way, the thrones of the Kingdom of the Netherlands and the Grand Duchy of Luxembourg were separated in 1890, with the succession of Princess Wilhelmina as the first Queen regnant of the Netherlands. As a remnant of Salic law, the office of the reigning monarch of the Netherlands is always formally known as 'King' even though her title may be 'Queen'. Luxembourg passed to the House of Orange-Nassau's distantly-related agnates, the House of Nassau-Weilburg. However, that house too faced extinction in the male line less than two decades later. With no other male-line agnates in the remaining branches of the House of Nassau, Grand Duke William IV adopted a semi-salic law of succession so that he could be succeeded by his daughters.

In the Channel Islands, the only part of the former Duchy of Normandy still held by the British Crown, Queen Elizabeth II is traditionally ascribed the title of Duke of Normandy (never Duchess). The influence of Salic law is presumed to explain why she is toasted as "The Queen our Duke". The same is the case in the Duchy and County Palatine of Lancaster, in England. The loyal toast there is to "The Queen, the Duke of Lancaster".

Literary references

Shakespeare uses the Salic Law as a plot device in *Henry V*, saying it was upheld by the French to bar Henry V's claiming the French throne. The play *Henry V* begins with the Archbishop of Canterbury being asked if the claim might be upheld despite the Salic Law. The Archbishop replies, "That the **land Salique** is in Germany, between the floods of Sala and of Elbe". The law is German, not French. The Archbishop's justification for Henry's claim, which Shakespeare intentionally renders obtuse and verbose (for comedic as well as politically expedient reasons), is also erroneous, as the Salian Franks originated in the Low Countries and the peoples of Clovis I lived along the Scheldt, in Belgium.

In the novel *Royal Flash*, by George MacDonald Fraser, the hero, Flashman, on his marriage, is presented with the Royal Consort's portion of the Crown Jewels, and "The Duchess did rather better"; the character, feeling hard done-by, thinks, "It struck me then, and it strikes me now, that the Salic Law was a damned sound idea".

In his novel *Waverley*, Sir Walter Scott quotes "Salique Law" when discussing the protagonist's prior requests for a horse and guide to take him to Edinburgh.

"The hostess, a civil, quiet, laborious drudge, came to take his orders for dinner, but declined to make answer on the subject of the horse and guide; for the Salique Law, it seems, extended to the stables of the Golden Candlestick." (Chapter XX1X)

Source http://en.wikipedia.org/wiki/Salic_law

Schwabenspiegel

The **Schwabenspiegel** is a legal code, written in ca. 1275 by a Franciscan friar in Augsburg. It deals mainly with questions of land ownership and fiefdom, and it is based on the Pentateuch, Roman law as well as Canon law. It draws on the early 13th century *Sachsenspiegel*, and is immediately dependent on the *Deutschenspiegel* code.

The name "mirror of the Swabians" is also taken from the *Sachsenspiegel* ("mirror of the Saxons"). Since the code is not prescriptive but descriptive, i.e. it records current legal practice, it does not impose any new laws, it was metaphorically compared to a mirror in which to perceive right and wrong.

Source http://en.wikipedia.org/wiki/Schwabenspiegel

Visigothic Code

The cover of an edition of the Liber Judiciorum from 1600.

The **Visigothic Code** (*Latin*, **Forum Iudicum** or **Liber Iudiciorum**; *Spanish*, **Libro de los Juicios**) comprises a set of laws promulgated by the Visigothic king of Hispania, Chindasuinth in his second year (642/643). They were enlarged by the novel legislation of Recceswinth (for which reason it is sometimes called the *Code of Recceswinth*), Wamba, Erwig, Egica, and perhaps Wittiza. In 654 Recceswinth promulgated the code anew after a project of editing by Braulio of Zaragoza, since Chindasuinth's original code had been quickly commissioned and enacted in rough.

They are often called the *Lex Visigothorum*, law of the Visigoths. However, this code abolished the old tradition of having different laws for Romans and for Visigoths; all the subjects of the kingdom would stop being *romani* and *gothi* to become *hispani*. In this way, all the subjects of the kingdom were gathered under the same jurisdiction, eliminating social apart from juridical differences.

The laws were far-reaching and long in effect: in 10th century Galicia, monastic charters make reference to the Code. The laws govern and sanction family life and by extension political life—the marrying and the giving in marriage, the transmission of property to heirs, the safeguarding of the rights of widows and orphans. Particularly with the Visigoth Law Codes, women could inherit land and title and manage it independently from their husbands or male relations, dispose of their property in legal wills if they had no heirs, and women could represent themselves and bear witness in court by age 14 and arrange for their own marriages by age 20.

The laws combine the Catholic Church's Canon law, and have a strongly theocratic tone.

The code is known to have been preserved by the Moors, as Christians were permitted the use of their own laws, where they did not conflict with those of the conquerors, upon the regular payment of tribute; thus it may be presumed that it was the recognized legal authority of Christian magistrates while the Iberian Peninsula remained under Muslim control. When Ferdinand III of Castile took Córdoba in the thirteenth century, he ordered the code to be adopted and observed by its citizens, and caused it to be rendered, albeit inaccurately, into Castilian, as the Fuero Juzgo. The Catalan translation of this document is the oldest literary text found in that language (c. 1150).

Contents

The following list has the book and titles from the Visigothic Code.

Book I: Concerning Legal Agencies
Title I: The Lawmaker
Title II: The Law
Book II: Concerning the Conduct of Causes
Title I: Concerning Judges, and Matters to be Decided in Court
Title II: Concerning Causes
Title III: Concerning Constituents and Commissions
Title IV: Concerning Witnesses and Evidence
Title V: Concerning Valid and Invalid Documents and How Wills Should be Drawn Up
Book III: Concerning Marriage
Title I: Concerning Nuptial Contracts
Title II: Concerning Unlawful Marriages
Title III: Concerning the Rape of Virgins, or Widows
Title IV: Concerning Adultery
Title V: Concerning Incest, Apostasy, and Pederasty
Title VI: Concerning Divorce, and the Separation of Persons who have been Betrothed
Book IV: Concerning Natural Lineage
Title I: Concerning the Degrees of Relationship
Title II: Concerning the Laws of Inheritance
Title III: Concerning Wards and Their Guardians
Title IV: Concerning Foundlings
Title V: Concerning Such Property as is Vested by the Laws of Nature
Book V: Concerning Business Transactions
Title I: Ecclesiastical Affairs
Title II: Concerning Donations in General
Title III: Concerning the Gifts of Patrons
Title IV: Concerning Exchanges and Sales
Title V: Concerning Property Committed to the Charge of, or Loaned to, Another
Title VI: Concerning Pledges and Debts
Title VII: Concerning the Liberation of

Slaves, and Freedmen
Book VI: Concerning Crimes and Tortures
Title I: Concerning the Accusers of Criminals
Title II: Concerning Malefactors and their Advisors, and Poisoners
Title III: Concerning Abortion
Title IV: Concerning Injuries, Wounds, and Mutilations, Inflicted upon Men
Title V: Concerning Homicide
Book VII: Concerning Theft and Fraud
Title I: Concerning Informers of Theft
Title II: Concerning Thieves and Stolen Property
Title III: Concerning Appropriators and Kidnappers of Slaves
Title IV: Concerning Forgers of Documents
Title V: Concerning Forgers of Documents
Title VI: Concerning Counterfeiters of Metals
Book VIII: Concerning Acts of Violence and Injuries
Title I: Concerning Attacks, and Plunder of Property
Title II: Concerning Arson and Incendiaries
Title III: Concerning injuries to Trees, Gardens, or Growing Crops of any Description
Title IV: Concerning Injury to Animals, and Other Property
Title V: Concerning the Pasturage of Hogs and Concerning Strays
Title VI: Concerning Bees, and the Damage They Cause
Book IX: Concerning Fugitives and Refugees
Title I: Concerning Fugitives, and Those who Conceal, and Assist Them in Their Flight
Title II: Concerning Those who Refuse to go to War, and Deserters
Title III: Concerning Those who Seek Sanctuary in a Church
Book X: Concerning Partition, Limitation, and Boundaries
Title I: Concerning Partition, and Lands Conveyed by Contract
Title II: Concerning the Limitations of Fifty and Thirty Years
Title III: Concerning Boundaries and Landmarks
Book XI: Concerning the Sick and the Dead and Merchants who Come from Beyond
Title I: Concerning Physicians and Sick Persons
Title II: Concerning Those who Disturb Sepulchres
Title III: Concerning Merchants who Come from Beyond Seas
Book XII: Concerning the Prevention of Official Oppression, and the Thorough Extinction of Heretical Sects
Title I: Concerning the Exercise of Moderation in Judicial Decisions, and the Avoiding of Oppression by Those Invested with Authority
Title II: Concerning the Eradication of the Errors of all Heretics and Jews
Title III: Concerning New Laws against the Jews, in which Old Ones are Confirmed, and New Ones are Added
Source http://en.wikipedia.org/wiki/Visigothic_Code